Creativity

A. J. CROPLEY, PH.D.

Assistant Professor of Psychology,
University of Saskatchewan, Regina Campus

LONGMAN

LONGMAN, GROUP LIMITED
London

Associated companies, branches and representatives throughout the world

First published 1967
Fourth impression 1971

ISBN 0 582 32057 7

Printed in Great Britain by
Lowe & Brydone (*Printers*) *Ltd*
London

Contents

Acknowledgements

The author first became interested in the topic of creativity while he was a student at the University of Alberta, Edmonton, Canada, and was particularly influenced, at the beginning, by Dr C. C. Anderson of that university. This interest was further stimulated by the opportunity to carry out some research in the area, which was afforded by the co-operation and assistance of various school officials, including Mr A. E. Hohol and Mr W. Klufas, both now of the Edmonton Public School Board. Thanks are due to these three people, and to the otherwise anonymous '320 Canadian grade seven children' who are mentioned frequently in the text. Dr Anderson got the author started along an interesting and rewarding line of inquiry, and the other 322 provided a fillip just when it was needed.

Introduction

The work of psychologists at about the turn of the present century, and especially the work of Binet, has left modern schoolteachers with a convention regarding human intellect which has only recently begun seriously to be questioned. In emphasising that individual differences could be measured by tests of judging and reasoning (rather than the tests of sensory acuity, psychomotor skills, and the like, which had previously been the basis of measurement of individual differences), Binet performed a work of unquestioned importance. However, later workers have tended to treat the particular kinds of tests which he employed, not as though they provide a useful approach to sampling human intellect, but as though the skills the tests measure define the limits of intellect. Hence, strictly logical reasoning, accompanied by accuracy, has come to be seen by some people as the *sine qua non* of effective intellectual functioning. Similarly, the IQ seems, to those same people, to be a thing or quantity which sums up all that needs to be known about an individual's intellect, rather than a numerical device useful in expressing the extent to which a person has responded to certain tests in a certain way.

The position adopted in this book is that intellect is not synonymous with the ability to respond in the usual logical and lawful way to a particular kind of test item. Furthermore, the IQ score is seen as merely a measure of the extent to which a person is capable of thinking in a certain way, a way characterised by its emphasis on logic and correctness, and usually aimed at finding a single best answer to any problem. Admittedly, the kinds of thinking which lead to high IQ scores tend to be closely related to success in our schools, and also correspond fairly well with the tendency to 'do well' in adult life, so that intelligence tests of the conventional kind are very useful indeed. The point is that the usefulness of these kinds of tests sometimes leads us to forget that they do, in fact, concentrate on one particular kind of thinking. On the other hand, some authors have recently focused attention on a different kind of thinking which involves chiefly the production of many and varied responses rather than the finding of single correct solutions, and have labelled it 'divergent thinking'. The more commonly used tests, which concentrate on logic and correctness, are said to measure mainly 'convergent thinking'. Thus, it is increasingly being suggested that intellect may manifest itself in at least two (and quite possibly more) different modes, one of which corresponds fairly well with what conventional IQ tests measure (convergent thinking) the other largely ignored (divergent thinking).

Along with this emphasis on the one-sidedness of conventionally used measures has come an increasing use of a kind of test which looks as though it measures something different from the skills sampled by IQ tests. These more recent tests are the so-called tests of creativity. As a matter of fact, no one is sure yet just what the defining properties of creativity are, and the ability of creativity tests to predict later levels of creativeness is unknown. One thing that is clear, however, is that human intellect can function in ways other than those elicited by the usual kinds of tests, and that other intellective modes can be elicited by different sorts of tests. Furthermore, the evidence is that people who do well on the conventional IQ tests do not always do as well on the newer tests, while some very capable people do not do at all well on conventional measures. The recent work of Hudson (1966) has demonstrated this point with particular force. Studying only schoolboys whose high capabilities had been demonstrated by superior school achievement, he showed that distinctions could be made among the boys on the basis of their preference for a divergent kind of thinking, on the one hand, or a convergent kind, on the other. If merely their IQ scores were taken into account, many of the superior students whom Hudson tested, among them some who went on to brilliant undergraduate careers, seemed unlikely candidates for success even at School Certificate level.

The success of such boys in the academic sphere despite low scores on conventional IQ tests strongly supports the view that such tests neither isolate all capable individuals, nor describe fully the limits of intellectual functioning. For these reasons, it seems desirable to look at some issues connected with creativity tests, particularly if their shortcomings are kept in mind as a safeguard against excessive enthusiasm. The purpose of the present book is certainly not to suggest that, in the concept of creativity, we do at last have the ultimate answer. Nevertheless, it is important that modern teachers should evaluate their students on as wide a basis as possible, and the concept of creativity, even in the limited sense in which the term is used here,[1] seems to be a step in the right direction.

In view of the complexity of the modern world it is increasingly important that teachers do not inhibit the development in their pupils of certain highly effective intellectual styles, merely because they differ from those traditionally regarded as important. Hence this book is concerned with demonstrating that there are quite able people whose intellectual *modus operandi* is divergent (creative, if you like), and that some of these people are badly underestimated by the kinds of tests usually used in measuring intellectual potential. This underestimation of certain people is a result of the fact that the commonly used tests concentrate on only one intellective mode.

The book is also concerned with demonstrating that differences in style of thinking between those who prefer the divergent mode and those who prefer the convergent appear to be related to differences between such individuals in the area of personality. People whose thinking is of the divergent kind display a consistent set of personality traits which include

[1] These limitations on the use of the term 'creativity' will be discussed more fully on pp. 7, 8.

characteristics like impulsiveness, non-conformity, willingness to 'have a go', and so on, while convergent thinkers are more likely to be impulse suppressing, conformist, and unwilling to let themselves go. Furthermore as a result of their characteristic life-style, highly creative children experience special relationships with their teachers, relationships which are not always to the children's advantage. Some details of the way creative children get on with their teachers are outlined in Chapter 5, and specific suggestions about how the teacher can utilise the divergent thinking skills of highly creative children are made in Chapter 6. Finally, Chapter 4 briefly reviews the kinds of parental practices which seem to be related to the appearance of divergent modes of thinking in children.

1

A Second Look at Intelligence Testing

Inadequacies of the IQ Concept

RECENT CHANGES IN THINKING ABOUT INTELLECTUAL ABILITY

The usual method employed in our schools when an estimate of a child's intellectual potential is needed has involved the use of conventional intelligence tests, and calculation of an IQ score. However, in recent years, the notion that the traditional kinds of intelligence tests have cornered the market on intellect, and that they measure all that is worth knowing about a child's intellectual functioning, has come under increasing fire. This dissatisfaction with the IQ concept in its present form is supported, for one thing, by the frequent failure of the usual kinds of tests to account for more than about one quarter of the variation in a class's scores on tests of classroom achievement, as Getzels and Jackson (1962, p.3) have pointed out. In fact, it has increasingly been argued that the kinds of intelligence tests commonly in use nowadays ignore important aspects of intellect. Furthermore, the neglected aspects are related, among other things, to performance in the classroom and are, therefore, of especial interest to teachers.

In particular, the recent increase in emphasis on aspects of intellect not sampled by traditional tests may be related to the work of Guilford (1950). He suggested that, whereas the usual kinds of tests concentrate on what he called 'convergent thinking', there are other effective but neglected intellective modes appropriately referred to as involving 'divergent thinking'. Convergent thinking is characterised by its dependence on reproduction of the already learned, and of fitting old responses to new situations in a more or less mechanical way, while divergent thinking, on the other hand, involves 'fluency, flexibility and originality' (Torrance, 1963, p.72), and is essentially concerned with the production of large numbers of new ideas. An almost identical point has been made by Bartlett (1958), who pointed out that intelligence tests, with their emphasis on correct solutions, elicit what he called 'closed thinking', and ignore 'open thinking'. Thus, the body of opinion which argues for the inadequacy of the commonly used IQ tests, stresses that such tests neglect thinking of the divergent, or open kind.

CONVENTIONAL TEST ITEMS

It is appropriate, at this point, to look closely at what is involved in traditional intelligence tests. They are usually group tests which require the subject to apply what he has learned in the past to a new problem, or which require him to abstract some rule from exemplars, and then reapply it. Usually there is only one correct answer to each problem and the tests can be scored simply by counting the number of correct responses. In this case, correctness is decided on the grounds of logic, arithmetical laws, grammatical laws, and the like. The child's job is to sort out the single correct answer which the rules dictate and, for these reasons, the tests are said to be convergent in content.

Thus, items might include ones like the following:

1. What number comes next in this series?
   2, 4, 8, 16, ?
2. Which word in the following list is least like 'new'?
   old, big, shiny, satisfactory.
3. Which of the following shapes is most like a triangle?
   circle, square, diamond, crescent.
   (This item is also suitable for non-verbal presentation.)

In question 1, the subject is required to abstract the rule that each number is twice the preceding one, and hence to conclude that the next number will be 32. Similarly, in question 2, he must notice that 'new' is an adjective which describes something's age, and hence conclude that it is exactly opposite to 'old' which is also an adjective describing age. Thus, 'old' resembles 'new' least. Finally, in question 3, he should notice that a triangle has straight lines for sides and also that it has angles which are not usually right angles, so that it is most like a diamond. In each case, he must respond to the item exactly as it is presented, must work out a conventional rule, and then must 'zero-in' on the best response.

A DIVERGENT APPROACH TO THE SAME ITEMS

However, the following possible lines of thought would lead to quite different answers to the three sample items. In the case of question 1, a subject might notice that the first three numbers would be written in a format uniform with that of 16 if they were written 02, 04, and 08 respectively. After this transformation of the test item, the first three numbers in the series all have zeroes in the tens position, so that probably the next three numbers should resemble each other in this respect too. Hence, the answer number ought to begin with 1, since 16 begins with a 1 in the tens column. Continuation of this line of reasoning might eventually lead to a completely different solution from '32' and the child would receive zero credit for that item.

The stimulus word in question 2 is 'new'. A child might reason as follows: 'New' tells about some condition of an object. So do 'old', 'shiny', and 'satisfactory'. 'Big' on the other hand describes size not state and is the only one of the words which has this sense. Therefore, the answer is 'big'. Finally in the case of question 3, a subject might observe that one frequently sees triangles on road signs. Another shape for road signs is the circle. Therefore, triangles and circles are closely related through their mutual membership in the class of shapes which are used for road signs, and the best answer is 'circle'. If this item were presented in a non-verbal form (i.e.

by showing a drawing of each shape), the logic of the road sign response would be particularly obvious. The child could simply draw in some details on the two shapes and label them both 'Sign'. In all three examples cited, the child concerned would receive no credit for his answers, and yet it is difficult to maintain that inferior thought processes have been utilised, although they are clearly different. It is such different kinds of thought processes with which this book is concerned.

WHAT CONVENTIONAL TESTS REQUIRE

In fact, most commonly used tests of the conventional kind call for the finding of a single correct response to a clearly defined and explicity stated test item. The main task facing the person taking such tests is to 'converge' upon that response which best fits the item—he may even be penalised and marked wrong for responding in an uncommon way, even though his response can be shown to be equally valid as the answer which the test manual labels the correct one. This sort of criticism is particularly true of mass-administered group tests of the pencil and paper kind. Basically, then, responses to this kind of test require the subject to recall the previously-learned and to recognise new examples of things he has seen before. Items are regarded as complete units in themselves, need no alteration or 'improvement' by the subject, and are solvable by the application of logic.

THEIR INAPPROPRIATENESS TO MODERN EDUCATION

Such tests are very well suited to the needs of an educational system whose main concern is the fostering of convergent thinking. Traditional tests are good predictors of performance when exams are chiefly concerned with testing the ability to regurgitate material acquired by rote. However, in the light of modern trends in education which have emphasised that learning by rote is, as Biggs (1965) for example has pointed out, inefficiently specific, wasteful of time and energy, the need today is for teaching which encourages children to acquire generalised learning strategies. Modern education must concern itself with developing not merely the rote-learning powers of students, but also their ability to produce relevant new codings of their classroom experiences, so that it is especially important that children's intellects function on as wide a basis as possible.

A NEW CONCEPT OF GIFTEDNESS

Thus, although in the past the concept of giftedness has usually been associated almost exclusively with high IQ, there is increasing recognition nowadays that IQ tests sample only a narrow band of intellectual skills. The most commonly used IQ tests are bound to traditional conceptions of the nature of intellectual functioning, and their validity is measured by comparing them with traditional tests like the Stanford-Binet. Such tests continue to measure what was measured by the older ones, and eliminate the possibility of measuring aspects of intellect which do not involve fixing on the most readily obvious answer in any test situation. Nowadays, however, alternative lines of reasoning which lead to quite different solutions like those described on page 3 are increasingly being recognised as important in assessing a child's intellectual potential.

The Concept of Divergent Thinking

ATTEMPTS TO ISOLATE DIVERGENT THINKING

Associated with this increasing recognition of the shortcomings of the traditional IQ concept way of looking at human intellectual ability—a way which may be summarised by saying that it assumes that intellect is limited to the kinds of abilities which lead to high scores in conventional tests—has come emphasis on divergent thinking and the search for 'pure' divergent thinking. Factor analysts have tried to show that divergent thinking tests measure unique aspects of intellect, or on the other hand that they do not; they have argued that general intelligence accounts for performance on both IQ-type tests and other intellectual tests (including those of the divergent type) or, conversely, that a special factor is needed to account for the way divergent tests relate to each other, and so on.

In fact, as the present author has pointed out in reporting some of his own research in this area (Cropley, 1966), the best compromise position between the two extremes proposed by the various factor analysts looks to be the view that intellectual functioning of the divergent kind is closely related to functioning of the convergent kind, although not by any means identical with it. In other words, people who tackle problems in a highly divergent way quite often get high scores on ordinary intelligence tests, but they may or may not do as well as they do on tests of the divergent kind. Some quite able people who possess high levels of divergent thinking skills may even do very badly on traditional intelligence tests, with the result that, although their intellectual style is highly effective in a divergent way, they may suffer the educational consequences of being labelled 'dull' or perhaps 'average'. To summarise all this plainly, some able people may prefer to function one way, some the other.[1]

However, the kinds of tests most commonly in use nowadays concentrate on skills of the convergent kind, and are sometimes unfair to those whose intellectual *modus operandi* is essentially divergent in form.

Possibly the most striking point about the search for a unique and distinct factor of divergent thinking is connected with the danger that the factor analysts are simply about to do the whole thing over again—the 'quotient hunt' is in danger of making people think of intellect as having two, and only two, modes which have been isolated factorially, may be tested usefully, and crystallise in their quotients all that is worth knowing about the intellect. Such a situation would

[1] It is important to notice that, in this conception, divergent thinking differs from convergent thinking in a qualitative rather than quantitative way. In other words, it is not more clever to be a divergent thinker than a convergent thinker, nor less clever. It is merely different.

scarcely be more desirable than the present position, and would represent an atomisation of human intellect, something which is better thought of as a complex entity functioning nevertheless in a highly unified way.

DIVERGENT THINKING AND CREATIVITY

A great deal of the recent work connected with divergent thinking has been reported by the authors concerned as involving investigation of creativity. However, in most cases, the independent variable has really been the tendency towards divergent thinking; to call such a tendency 'creativity' is of doubtful validity.

In fact, very little is known about creativity. Just what is creative, and what conventional, differs from culture to culture and from time to time, so that different authors have employed different criteria in selecting highly creative individuals. Freud (1910) and Sharpe (1950), for example, studied persons generally acclaimed for 'creative eminence', Eiduson (1958) identified highly creative individuals by their pursuit of acknowledged 'creative' activities, while Rossman (1931), Clifford (1958), and Drevdahl and Cattell (1958) employed, as a criterion of creativity, the extent to which their subjects had published works like books or pieces of sculpture. Hence, there is no consensus concerning just how creativity is to be recognised. Furthermore, nobody knows whether divergent thinking tests predict creative behaviour in later life, in the same way as IQ tests predict academic achievement and 'doing well' in life, and until an investigation like Terman's (1925) study of intelligence is carried out, this point will remain unclear.

Thus, it is very important to notice at this juncture that the term 'creativity' is coming to have a highly circumscribed meaning in the field of psychological measurement, although it is still used in a very loose way by some psychologists. In its strictly psychometric sense the word is emptied of the social, aesthetic, and professional connotations which are connected with its everyday use, although, of course, the 'scientific' use of the term does not preclude the possibility that creativity tests are related to creative behaviour in later life. Hence, although the concept of creativity is a difficult one to employ with precision because of its impreciseness, the term is coming to be accepted by many psychologists and educators as referring to an intellective mode characterised by thinking of the divergent kind. In the sense that the term is used in this book, then, creativity means something very like what Guilford refers to as 'divergent thinking', or Bartlett as 'open thinking', rather than what the layman has in mind when he uses the term. This 'tougher' use of the word is preferred because it is more objective than the everyday sense in which the term is employed, and because it does not make the assumption that a preference for the divergent mode of thinking is necessarily directly related to creativity in the aesthetic and professional sense. Furthermore, it avoids problems associated with differences between cultures, differences from time to time within a culture, and differences across the various levels of a particular culture, which are inherent in the colloquial use of the term.

In fact, the similarity between the concept of creativity as it is used in this book, and divergent thinking, is close enough for the two terms to be used almost interchangeably, although this is a result of limitations placed on the use of creativity, rather than an assumption that divergent thinking is necessarily a predictor of later creativeness. The present author would prefer to use the notion of divergent thinking exclusively, since this avoids any possibility of confusion between the everyday conception of what 'creativity' means, and the strict psychometric meaning of the term, according to which it is a shorthand for referring to the fact that certain tests go together. However, the term 'creativity' is a very meaningful one, and is by now so well established in the literature and so widely used that strict insistence on the exclusive use of 'divergent thinking' would involve restating the findings of almost all research in the area, and would be unnecessarily pedantic in the present context. As long as the reader bears in mind the fact that it is not known whether, say, Michaelangelo or Einstein would have done well on these tests, it is legitimate to refer to them generically as 'creativity tests'.

RESISTANCE TO THE STUDY OF CREATIVITY

In the recent upsurge of interest in creativity, many teachers have been reminded of a point of view that was prominent a few years ago. According to this notion, the classroom teacher had to be very careful when he dealt with any impertinent, disobedient, untidy, or otherwise troublesome child in his class. A firm attempt to stem the undesirable behaviour of the class trouble-maker, the teacher was told, involved crushing the little fellow's natural creativeness. Most teachers reacted strongly against the argument that troublesome children should be handled with tolerance as their only offence lay in being highly creative, and they were quite right to do so. Behavioural disorders may stem from various emotional upsets, and it is perfectly proper for the teacher to appreciate that disorderly behaviour often has deep-seated roots which do not lie in a sheer natural bent for mischief-making. However, it is quite wrong to suppose that the troublesome student is by definition 'creative' and conversely, that the creative child need of necessity be troublesome.

The following two case studies demonstrate that there is something wrong with the present IQ concept. At the same time, they go a long way toward meeting the traditionalists' objection that the divergent thinker is little better than a downright nuisance in the classroom.

A Case Study of a Highly Intelligent Schoolboy

SELECTION

In 1948, 240 boys ranging in age from eleven years to fifteen years, were given a battery of intelligence and achievement tests in order to sort them out for streaming purposes. They were all beginning students in a large metropolitan high school in a large Australian city. One boy was placed second on the whole battery, and had the highest IQ of any boy tested that year—160 plus. This was Tom, the subject of the first case study. At the present time Tom is a mature man, and has now passed his thirtieth birthday. He was selected for study rather than a more recent student so that his progress through school and university could be examined in detail.

TOM

At the time at which the test data was collected, Tom was a schoolboy aged eleven years one month. He was about to enter the eighth class in the school system in which he was educated, and had achieved this advanced status at the age of eleven by 'skipping' grades along the way. He was, in fact, a full two years younger than the average age of his classmates. He was a smallish, slightly overweight boy, very shy and totally uninterested in sport. His smallness was exaggerated by his comparative youth, and physically he was a sound specimen. Both his parents were graduates and had lived apart for several years. Tom liked listening to classical music, but detested 'modern' music. His favourite school subject was hard to choose as he liked them all, but it was probably mathematics. His hobby was chess. Although he did not like sport, and was no good at it, he was prepared to do his best in inter-class games.

TOM'S PERSONALITY STRUCTURE

No more or less 'objective' personality assessment is available for Tom, and the following remarks are based upon observation of him in uncontrolled situations. He was extremely shy and timorous, causing his playmates a great deal of embarrassment by the rapidity with which he was reduced to tears. Otherwise he kept his feelings very much to himself and had virtually no really close friends. This state of affairs continued right throughout his school and university days.

He was extremely ambitious and very hard working. He was ego-involved with his performance in school and would sulk for days, or even cry, if he did badly in a test. His level of expectation of himself was so high that he regarded less than 100 per cent as a failure.

TOM AS HIS TEACHERS SAW HIM

Although they tended to describe him as a 'bit of a baby' and mostly admitted that they could not really get to like him as a person, Tom's teachers talked enthusiastically when asked about him. He was invariably described as a 'pleasure to teach', 'a willing and able boy', 'an ornament to the classroom', and so on. He was obedient and well-behaved and was, you might say, the apple of his teachers' eyes. His best subjects were maths, science, and Latin, while he produced grammatically perfect, stylistically dull work for his English teacher, who found him word perfect but uninspired.

TOM'S PARENT'S CHILD-REARING PRACTICES

Tom had been raised from an early age by his mother alone. She was an energetic woman who dominated the boy at all times. She told him when he might play, when he must do homework, when he must read 'good' novels, and so on. She insisted that he must play chess with her at a given time each evening, insisted on a certain schedule for piano practice (Tom played mechanically—technically well, but lifelessly), and ran his life completely. She administered severe corporal punishment for trivial offences, and was, overall, domineering, controlling, intrusive, and authoritarian.

TOM'S INTELLECTUAL FUNCTIONING

Tom was a brilliant student. As his high school career progressed, he went from success to success. He topped his entire state in every public exam for which he sat, and invariably carried off first place in most individual subjects, although he was never near the top in English. He did not take any subjects like art, but concentrated on more 'academic' courses. He matriculated too young for admission to a university and was obliged to spend an extra year at school, during which he took up several entirely new subjects at sixth form level and handled them with ease in one year instead of six or seven. He easily won a university place on the basis of his second set of what were essentially A level results, although he had only taken up the subjects for which he sat, one year previously. His career through university was similarly brilliant and he gained first or second place every year in every subject. At present, he is a professional man in an Australian city, and he is doing well. It is interesting to notice that he is merely at the middle of his profession, and has failed to make the same kind of mark as he did when he was a student. He has made no contribution, either theoretical or empirical, to his profession.

SUMMARY REMARKS ABOUT TOM

Tom is a good extreme example of the kind of person who performs at the highest levels on measures of IQ and the like, and does brilliantly in academic pursuits, but who shows little evidence of creativity. His level of aspiration was very high indeed, and his interests were strictly confined to lawful and logical convergent pursuits like mathematics and chess. What evidence there is concerning his levels of divergent thinking suggests that he operated in a highly convergent way. His English essays were wooden and stilted, although grammatically perfect; he ignored any creative pursuits; he played the piano only because his mother forced him to, played mechanically and hated it.

His mother was domineering, non-egalitarian, and punitive. She was unwilling to grant him any independence at all. Tom was inept in handling other people, introverted, shy and unable to express emotions except when they built up until he was overwhelmed in a flood of tears or a burst of rage. He was unable to find any interest in sport, was very shy with girls and had virtually nothing to do with them (he was still unmarried at thirty). In summary then, Tom was an outstanding scorer on IQ tests, was a dedicated and brilliant student of subject areas which involved lawfulness and logic, and displayed very low levels of divergent thinking. Thus, he is a good example of the kind of person who is very high on intelligence and very low on creativity.[1]

The following section is concerned with a case study of a highly creative student. The differences between Tom and Kathy, the subject of the second study, illustrate with particular force many of the important points about the highly creative thinker.

A Case Study of a Highly Creative Schoolgirl

SELECTION PROCEDURE

In 1964, the Minnesota Tests of Creative Thinking were administered to some 200 high school children in a large Australian country town, and the children's responses scored for Originality of Figures and Originality of Titles. One girl obtained the highest score on both dimensions. The extent to which her scores on the creativity battery were outstanding can be seen from the fact that not only was she the highest scorer on both dimensions, but her scores on the two creativity measures were not even approached in a survey of similar students at two other rural high schools. She scored 57 for Originality of Figures, compared with an average score of 29·4 for the whole group, and she scored 88 for Originality of Titles, almost four times the average score of 22·2. This was Kathy, the subject of the present case study.[2]

[1] It is important to notice that both students described in these two case studies represent extremes, one of intelligence unaccompanied by divergent thinking, the other of divergence but not commensurately high IQ. Most people will fall somewhere between these two types.

[2] The author wishes to express his gratitude to Mr Paul Johnson, who was responsible for both the design of the case study, and also for the collection and analysis of the data reported.

KATHY

At the time of the study, Kathy was an attractive, rather sophisticated girl, aged sixteen years one month. She has an older brother and an older sister who are both seeking further education. Her parents belong to the minor professions and have both had some university training. Kathy's interests include art, sculpture and music, although she is also a keen sportswoman, and is very interested in social contacts with boys. She likes classical music, folk music and jazz, too, and her main hobbies are playing the guitar (folk music), playing the piano, and collecting art prints. Her favourite school subject is art, which she is taking at advanced level. When she leaves school she hopes to become an art teacher.

DATA FROM THE SCHOOL RECORD CARD

Kathy's IQ was 119, derived from a verbal score of 113 and a number score of 121. Specific abilities, expressed in such a form that average ability=5 (SD=1), included non-verbal ability 5·9, speed and accuracy 6·2, and perceptual and spatial ability 6·5. Although these scores indicate that Kathy is of high average IQ, and has a number of well-developed specific abilities, her scores on conventional tests are by no means commensurate with her creativity scores. These latter scores suggest that she is perhaps one in a thousand as far as divergent thinking is concerned, while her IQ scores place her as merely one in six or thereabouts.

KATHY'S PERSONALITY STRUCTURE

The Rorschach test was administered to Kathy and the data interpreted 'blind', by an independent rater who had no personal knowledge of who Kathy was or of why she was being tested. This 'blind' rating of the Rorschach is important, because it eliminates the possibility that interpretations were influenced by prior knowledge of what it was hoped the test would reveal.

The interpretation of the Rorschach data indicated that Kathy is essentially a theoretical type, but that she retains reasonable contact with the practical requirements of a situation. She revealed a sensitive self-awareness and a need for warm personal relationships, accompanied by a tendency for free emotional expression and a tendency for uncontrolled emotion. Nevertheless, she is essentially an extraverted person, despite her interest in her own emotions, and her willingness to express them freely. Finally, responses to the test indicated that she is ambitious and can push herself hard in her school work in seeking success.

KATHY AS HER TEACHERS SAW HER

Kathy's various teachers were asked to report on her as a pupil and also as a person. Her teachers in mathematics and science reported that she was normal in her classroom behaviour and that she was not excessively noisy or inattentive. Her science teacher commented on her tendency to get very enthusiastic about portions of the course and to put an unusual amount of work into anything which caught her imagination (for example, a project in geology which the teacher cited). This teacher also commented on Kathy's high levels of initiative and drive.

The French teacher found Kathy friendly and respectful, and commented favourably on her positive personality. This point was also emphasised by the teacher who took her for English and history. This teacher mentioned that Kathy 'has definite opinions on things' and that she possessed 'a strong personality'. Although opportunities for creative work were limited at the level at which Kathy was studying, her English teacher was particularly struck by the high quality of her creative production, and commented too on her eagerness to 'delve into things'. All teachers were satisfied with Kathy's school work and rated it 'good' or 'satisfactory'.

It was the comments of Kathy's art teacher which were really enthusiastic. This teacher described her as outstanding. She was 'a rewarding child to teach' and was 'creative with an all round talent in art'. These comments echoed the report of Kathy's capacities which had accompanied her on her move to high school from her primary school. On the report, she was described as 'artistic, reliable, versatile'.

KATHY'S PARENTS' ATTITUDES TO CHILD-REARING

An inventory was administered to Kathy's parents, in an attempt to assess their views on child-rearing. The inventory was developed by Schaeffer and Bell in 1958. Her parents' responses to this inventory indicated that they believed strongly in fostering egalitarianism, comradeship, and approval of her activities, while they were strongly opposed to fostering dependency, breaking the will, and intrusiveness. Hence her parents tended to be egalitarian and permissive. They encouraged independence and tried to share in the child's interests, while they avoided prying into her affairs any more than was absolutely necessary, and made no attempt to break her will or to make her dependent upon them.

SUMMARY REMARKS ABOUT KATHY

This then was Kathy. The evidence of the two creativity scores was borne out by the comments of her art teacher, and by her primary school report. She was a highly creative girl, quite outstanding in art and interested in activities of an 'artistic' kind. The other aspects of her life may thus be considered for the light they cast on the nature of the highly creative person. She was a sensitive and likeable girl, who was hard-working, well-behaved, and respectful, yet possessed of a mind of her own. Despite her artistic interests, she was also an enthusiastic basket-baller, and enjoyed social contacts with boys. Her relationships with her parents were good, and she was well liked by her teachers, even the ones for whom her work was merely satisfactory. She was accustomed to giving expression to her emotions but, at the same time, firmly in touch with reality and in control when control became necessary. Her IQ was good average for children in the academic stream at the upper high school level, and her general school work was of a similar standard.

A picture of Kathy emerges from the case study which is very different from the stereotype of the creative child held by many teachers. She was nothing like the unruly, impertinent trouble-maker that some teachers think of when the term creativity is used. On the other hand, she was by no means the unworldly dreamer of the opposite stereotype held by some other people. She was active and alert, realistic and ambitious, and thoroughly able to control her own emotions while at the same time not at all afraid to express them. In her relations with other people she was skilful and warm, although she sometimes seemed shy when she felt she was being evaluated. She was neither the undisciplined Beatnik of the one stereotype, nor the 'tender flower' of the other.

Summary

A COMPARISON OF TOM AND KATHY

The case studies given in this chapter describe two very able youngsters of markedly different intellectual styles. In fact, the compelling intellectual differences between the two students are by no means an isolated instance of two capable children whose intellectual functioning differs diammetrically: Hudson (1966) has reported a large number of cases of able boys who could be paired in the same way, some preferring the convergent style, some the divergent, and the reader who wishes to pursue the point should look at his book.

If one re-examines the data about Tom and Kathy, several clear cut differences emerge. The most compelling of these, of course, involves the striking intellectual differences between them. However, differences between the two children were by no means confined to the intellectual domain. These intellectual differences were accompanied by differences on a number of non-intellective variables and some of these may even play a causal role in the intellectual differences. One important non-intellective difference centred around the different child-rearing practices of the two sets of parents. Tom's mother was punitive and domineering, and completely destroyed her son's independence and spirit. She drove him to achieve outstanding performance in academic pursuits, and regulated all his spare time. On the other hand, Kathy's parents were permissive, and fostered independence in their daughter. Although these two students are extreme examples, there is a good deal of evidence to suggest that there is a systematic relationship between parental practices in rearing their children and the degree of creativity manifested by those children. The essential differences between parents of the two kinds of thinkers are typified by the differences between Tom's mother and Kathy's. This point will be developed more fully in Chapter 4.

Similarly, the differences in the capacities of the two young people to handle their own emotions is very clear cut. Tom never showed emotion, except when it was out of control. At other times he kept it bottled up. On the other hand, Kathy expressed emotion freely and yet in a controlled way. In their relationships with other people too, they were more or less polar opposites. Tom was socially inept, Kathy was very skilled indeed. Again, these differences in personality between the highly creative Kathy and the highly intelligent Tom will be discussed in detail in a later chapter.

Hence, although a reaction against the notion that the classroom trouble-maker is the kind of person the psychologist has in mind when he talks about creativity has led some teachers completely to discount the study of creativity, there is a good deal of evidence nowadays that:

1 There is an aspect of intellect which may appropriately be labelled creativity, provided that the shortcomings of the term are kept in mind.
2 This aspect of intellect can be estimated by appropriate tests.
3 There is a significant relationship between creativity and academic achievement.
4 Highly creative children tend to have a special relationship

with their parents. The tendency to think divergently is related to parental child-rearing practices.

5 Appropriate teaching methods can encourage children to think creatively, or discourage them from doing so.

Why Study Creativity?

Furthermore, the study of the inventive and innovative aspects of human intellect is so important today that it has been described by Bruner (1962) as restoring dignity to the human being in a computer dominated age, and by Toynbee (1962) as a vital aspect of a nation's resources. More and more, modern man is finding that routine tasks have been taken over by automated procedures—in teaching, the rise of programmed instruction methods is one example of this kind of development. To some people, the electronic computer almost seems to be 'thinking' these days, and even tasks which have not previously been regarded as routine have been reduced to that status by the advances in technology which have been an important aspect of modern progress. Short of procreation of the species, there seem to be few tasks which computers cannot, or will not soon be able to do, faster and better than human beings, and some thinkers have turned to creativity as the last stronghold of human dignity.

Moreover, in the light of the 'knowledge explosion' which is taking place nowadays, and the consequent need for ever wider use of human scientific and technological ingenuity, it has become essential that a nation make the best possible use of all its intellectual resources if it is even to maintain its position in the modern world. It may well be that the nation which emerges from the next few decades in the most desirable position will be the one which does this best. We are in the middle of a 'brains race' nowadays which has made the process of education a matter of increasing importance to the community. Thus, the role of the teacher in freeing his students to function at their maximum capacity is a vital one. For this reason, the remainder of this book will be devoted to an examination of the issues raised on page 18.

2

Creativity and Classroom Achievement

What is Creativity?

FREQUENT MISCONCEPTIONS

In attempting to say what we mean when we talk about creativity, it is important that one thing be made quite clear, right from the start. Terms like 'creativity' are used far too loosely in everyday conversation, and (when used by some people) have come to mean nothing more than doing whatever you like, or behaving in an undisciplined way. It is quite wrong to suppose that this is what a psychologist means when he talks about creativity. It is true that divergent behaviour often seems to involve impulse expression, but this is far from meaning that expressing impulses is synonymous with being creative. As Kneller (1965) has pointed out, mere uninhibited hipswivelling can scarcely be called creative dancing, nor can hurling splashes of paint at canvas in random arrangement be regarded in itself as artistic creativity.

Similarly, some people mistakenly imagine that mere unconventionality is in itself creative, or that merely to do something differently from most people around you is to be a divergent thinker. On the contrary, if one accepted this notion, madness would be the most prolific source of creativity yet known. It is quite possible that a divergent individual may be unconventional; the point is that it is not the unconventionality which makes him creative. At the most, the unconventionality is an accompaniment to the creative process, and not really part of it.

Often, too, some of the qualities which are helpful in being a creative thinker are mistaken for creativity itself. Thus, creative thinking is often confused with quick-wittedness, or highly developed verbal skill or other such attributes which Kneller (1965, p.2) has called 'pointers to creativity, rather than the thing itself'. This kind of error can be harmful to the individual wrongly labelled 'creative' on the grounds that he displays a few of the fringe qualities of the true divergent thinker, for it may lead him to believe that creativity is mainly a matter of giving oneself cheap satisfactions without careful judgment of one's own behaviour. It is wrong to suppose that creative productions result from the mere scrapping of the conventional and consequent blind unconventionality.

One of the most important things about creativity is that it should lead to worthwhile results. These results may even have a kind of compelling property about them which identifies them immediately to the knowledgeable observer, sometimes with a distinct shock of recognition. Often this recognition of the obvious power of a truly creative act is accompanied by an experience of the 'Now why didn't I think of that?' kind, or by a real pleasure and excitement. Even in so staid a situation as a chess match, for instance, spectators in Imperial Russia are supposed to have showered the contestants with gold and even wept for joy when a particularly creative move was made. Kneller (1965, p.6) refers to this compelling quality as 'relevance', while Bruner (1962) has made the point particularly well by saying that a defining attribute of the creative production is that it is 'effective'. In some creative people, the search for effective end-products is so compelling that it shows up in a sense of complete dedication.

Classroom Effectiveness of Creative Individuals

CREATIVE AND INTELLIGENT INDIVIDUALS NOT THE SAME

If effectiveness and relevance are really important aspects of creative thinking, creative children ought to demonstrate their intellectual effectiveness in the classroom situation by superior academic attainment. The remainder of this chapter concerns this point. First of all, it should be pointed out that if scores on intelligence tests coincided with creativity scores, there would really be no point in investigating any relationship between creative thinking and achievement, since IQ achievement studies would have done the job already. In fact, selection of the top groups on the basis of IQ alone omits many highly capable students, especially among those who score very high on creativity tests (e.g. Kathy). Hence, groups of high IQ children contain neither all bright children nor all highly creative individuals.

The inability of IQ tests to select all intellectually superior children has been demonstrated repeatedly in the case studies reported by Hudson (1966), while Torrance (1962) has emphasised with particular clarity their inability to isolate highly creative children. He pointed out that the use of IQ as the sole criterion of giftedness, although this is the traditional practice, may well be a seriously defective technique. The top 20 per cent of the school population on the basis of IQ alone tends to include only about 30 per cent of those individuals who are in the top 20 per cent on measures of creative thinking. In fact, then, the group traditionally regarded as containing the gifted overlooks about 70 per cent of the highly creative.

Torrance's point is supported by an examination of Kathy's scores on the various tests of intellectual functioning which she took. Her IQ was recorded as 119, or about ten points above the average IQ for children at her level of schooling in New South Wales. This means that although she was an above-average student on the basis of IQ, she was not in the top 20 per cent. Her verbal IQ was only 113, so that she was barely above average as far as that score was concerned. Thus, selection of the top 20 per cent of students on the basis of IQ alone would not have included Kathy. In fact, if verbal IQ were the criterion, she would not merely be excluded from the top 20 per cent but would barely be included in the top 50 per cent. The inappropriateness of such an exclusion is very strongly emphasised when one examines her scores on the creativity tests. With creativity as the selection criterion, far from not making the top 20 per cent, Kathy scored at least at the 99th percentile. In other words, she was in the top 1 per cent or less of her peer group, as far as creativity was concerned, but far below it on the basis of IQ.

GROUPING STUDIES RELATING CREATIVITY TO ACADEMIC ACHIEVEMENT

Getzels and Jackson (1962) focused attention on this relationship when they selected two groups of children which they labelled 'High IQ' and 'High Creative' respectively. The first group consisted of children in the top 20 per cent on IQ but not on creativity, while the second group contained those children in the top 20 per cent on creativity but not on IQ. Although the intelligent group had a mean IQ twenty-three points above that of the creative group, there were no significant differences in academic achievement between the two. Consequently it was implied that creativity can compensate in some way for relative lack of skill in the areas sampled by more conventional intelligence tests. However, the sample of children studied by those two authors was a particularly unrepresentative one, consisting as it did of children who were enrolled in the University of Chicago School. For example, the mean IQ for the whole student enrolment of 449 was 132, while the High Creative Group, which was selected in such a way as to exclude students of really high IQ, nevertheless had a mean IQ of 127.

Hence there is some doubt concerning the extent to which the Getzels–Jackson findings can be taken to reflect the state of affairs in schoolchildren as a whole. For example, in most classrooms their pupils of relatively low IQ would be considered very bright children. Consequently various researchers have tried to verify the relationship suggested by those two workers. Torrance (1960) has conducted no fewer than eight replicatory studies which avoided some of the Getzels–Jackson shortcomings. Thus, in six studies conducted in elementary schools, the mean IQ of the highly divergent thinkers (which does not include the top 20 per cent on IQ) ranged from 97·9 to 126·5. In four of the six elementary school studies, Torrance found that there were no significant differences in overall academic achievement between the High IQ Group and the High Creative Group, and he made similar findings in the case of both samples of university students which he studied.

Yamamoto (1964a) also compared the academic performance of secondary school children selected in the way described by Getzels and Jackson. He obtained results which he described as 'clear cut'. Despite IQ differences of twenty points, the divergent thinking group did as well on the Iowa Tests of Educational Development, as did the High IQ Group. This finding was true both for boys and girls separately, and also when both sexes were combined. In a second study Yamamoto (1964b)[1] compared the achievement scores of a High Creative Group with those of a Low Creative Group allowing for differences in IQ between the two groups. Hence, he posed the question: 'Do children who score high on tests of creativity do better on classroom achievement than children who score low on such tests, after differences in IQ have been allowed for?' His results showed that the highly creative thinkers surpassed the low creative children, and from this he concluded that there were differences in achievement between the highly divergent thinkers and the uncreative students which were not due to differences in IQ. These differences led Yamamoto to the notion that there is a distinct relationship between performance on creativity tests and success in school learning.

The present author, too, has investigated the extent to which creativity scores are related to school achievement. In a study based on 320 Canadian children (Cropley, 1967) he selected four groups of children, on the following bases: The first group (the High-High Group) consisted of those children in the top half on both creativity and IQ, the second group (the Low-Low Group) consisted of those children in the lower half

[1] Yamamoto, K., 'A further analysis of the role of creative thinking in high school achievement', *Journal of Psychology*.

on both measures, while the third and fourth groups contained those children high on IQ but not on creativity (the High-Low Group), and low on IQ but high on creativity (the Low-High Group), respectively.[1] If creativity does add importantly to academic success, and creativity scores discriminate significantly between those likely to achieve highly and those likely to do less well, it should be possible to discriminate between high and low achievers, on the basis of creativity scores, even after IQ differences have been removed. Thus, among the highly intelligent, those who are highly creative should surpass those who are low on creativity, while among the less intelligent, once again the highly creative should surpass those who are low on both quantities. Hence, it would be expected that the High-High group would achieve significantly better than the High-Low group, despite the absence of IQ differences, and similarly, that the Low-High group would surpass the Low-Low group, again despite the absence of differences in IQ. Both of these expectations were borne out: in fact, the mean achievement scores formed an ordered sequence in descending order, with the High-Highs averaging 69·6 per cent, the High-Lows 63·5 per cent, the Low-Highs 56·6 per cent, and the Low-Lows 51·9 per cent. Thus, although the group high only on intelligence surpassed both low IQ groups as might be expected, the intellectual 'all-rounders' (high on both kinds of thinking) did best of all.

IMPLICATIONS OF FINDINGS FOR CONCEPTS OF OVER- AND UNDER-ACHIEVEMENT

The results cited above are particularly interesting if they are considered in the light of the notions of over- and under-achievement. Presumably, the High-Low group, whose mean IQ was 124, would be described by their teachers as under-achieving, since, despite the possession of equally high IQs, they failed to do as well on their school exams as did the High-High group (mean IQ 128). Similarly, the Low-High

[1] This study is described in greater detail in Appendix A.

group would probably be regarded as over-achievers, since, despite relatively low IQ (mean IQ for this group was 105), they achieved at a significantly higher level than did the Low-Lows who were of similar IQ (mean IQ 101).

In fact, several authors have pointed out that so-called 'over-achievers' might be better thought of as merely under-estimated by the tests employed, while under-achievers may more meaningfully be thought of as overestimated by the tests used to assess their potential. The data presented here support this notion, and suggest that IQ alone is an inadequate predictor of academic success; at the very least, further discrimination between those who achieve at high levels and those who do less well can be effected by the use of creativity scores.

CORRELATIONAL STUDIES

In the present author's study, described above, correlations were also calculated between the six divergent thinking tests employed and the academic achievement scores. The correlation coefficients obtained ranged from ·163 to ·420 when all children were considered, regardless of their grouping on the joint IQ–Creativity basis. Torrance (1959) reported similar findings with a sample of seventy-five children ranging from grade 4 to grade 6 in their educational level. The correlation coefficients he obtained ranged from ·37 to ·53 and, even when the effect of IQ was removed, the subsequent partial correlations were still as large as ·23 to ·48. Finally, Cline, Richards and Needham (1963) demonstrated that scores on creativity tests correlated significantly with high school science marks. Hence, correlation studies, too, indicate that there are significant relationships between divergent thinking and classroom achievement.

Classroom Skills Related to Creativity

DIFFERENTIAL IMPORTANCE OF CREATIVITY

In the previous section, examination of the relationship

between creativity and achievement was largely confined to consideration of global achievement scores based on a range of school subjects. For example, the achievement score employed in the present author's research was based on what the Canadians called 'core courses', and included marks for English, science, mathematics, and social studies. However, it is commonly accepted nowadays that the mental abilities sampled by various tests of the 'convergent' kind (IQ tests) are of differing importance in different kinds of achievement. Thus, a verbal IQ test is expected to be more useful in predicting success in verbal tasks than in performance tasks, and so on. In a similar way, it seems likely that the skills sampled by divergent tests should be more important in some kinds of classroom achievement than in others.

Torrance (1962a, pp.59-62) has discussed this point in some detail, and has reported the results of studies in five U.S. elementary schools in which the mean achievement of High IQ and High Creative groups of schoolchildren was compared in four subject areas. On the basis of his data, he concluded that highly creative students tend to do better in reading and language skills, despite IQ differences which were as large, in some cases, as 26. In the case of students at university level, the highly creative students tended to surpass the high IQ groups on measures like creative applications and self-initiated learning, again despite large intelligence differences in favour of the high IQ groups.

Correlational data, too, suggest that high levels of creativity are differently related to success in different subject areas. Thus, for example, Torrance (1962a, p.63) reports partial correlations (with the effect of IQ removed) of ·48 between creativity and reading skill, and only ·28 between creativity and arithmetic skill. Hence, the conclusion may be drawn that creativity scores are particularly related to achievement in language tests, and least related to achievement in arithmetical tests. This is not altogether unexpected, if one keeps in mind the differences between the kinds of questions usually comprising the two sorts of tests. Arithmetic tests, in particular, often emphasise the finding of single correct solutions through the application of previously learned techniques and may, therefore, be heavily convergent in nature.

The most recent research in this area has been reported by Hudson (1966). In a series of studies covering several years and involving several hundred boys of proven academic ability, he investigated relationships between academic achievement and intellectual style. He was interested in the extent to which stylistic biases in the boys' profiles on a number of ability measures, including IQ, accuracy, vocabulary, general knowledge and expressed interests, were reflected in their preference for arts- or science-type subjects. He showed that it was possible, by looking at the patterns of scores, to sort the boys into those with an 'arts bias' and those with a 'science bias'. This finding indicates that success in a particular subject area is closely related to an individual's intellectual style or, as Hudson (1966, p.30) puts it: 'the academically successful boy is distinguished not by his intellectual apparatus, but by the use he sees fit to make of it'.

On the basis of this evidence, Hudson examined the divergent/convergent thinking dichotomy as one major way of conceptualising differences in intellectual style, and he obtained results which will be seen by some people as rather surprising. Divergent thinkers showed an overwhelming preference for arts subjects (in other words, they preferred literature, modern languages, history, art and the like), while convergent thinkers strongly preferred science subjects (maths, physical sciences and so on). Thus, Hudson's research adds strong support to the idea that preference for a divergent mode of thinking is reflected in a particular pattern of school achievement.

The Role of Creativity in Achievement

CONVENTIONAL INTELLIGENCE AS THE BASIS FOR CREATIVITY

Different authors have suggested differing ways in which creativity may facilitate academic achievement, and one highly plausible suggestion has been proposed by authors like Bruner

(1962) and Pribram (1964). This is the notion of conventional convergent-type thinking as providing an essential foundation on which the divergent thinker builds. This point of view is implicit in the suggestion by Bruner that creative solutions can only occur when the relevant field of subject matter is thoroughly known. He has argued that the major kind of intellectual behaviour consists in reorganising data input from the external world, in such a way as to reduce the 'cognitive strain' (1963, p.134) of information processing. This data reorganisation is essentially a process of grouping data into categories, on the basis of their being operationally identical (i.e., for all practical purposes the same), and is called 'coding'. Creative thinking occurs when the codings resulting from this process of combination possess the property of 'effectiveness' and 'surprise'. However, the combinations (codings) of data are far from random. They are, in fact, informed by the coder's previous experience; they are not blind stabs, but effective insights based on knowledge of the subject matter involved and of the relevant rules of the game. Hence, in this way, Bruner has stressed the importance of conventional intelligence (convergent thinking) in the effecting of divergent breakthroughs.

Gordon too (1961, p.9) has stressed the importance of thorough knowledge of material in creativity, and he doubts that the 'moment of insight' mentioned, for example, by Ghiselin (1955, pp.29, 30) occurs in isolation. It seems most likely, to him, to arise out of thorough familiarity with the field. Pribram (1964, pp.107-8) has further emphasised this point of view by arguing that original productions do not arise by chance, but that they represent an extension of the already known. Hence, he emphasises strongly that creativity arises out of conventional intelligence—the 'work' involved in thinking divergently is concerned with extending the boundaries of the conventional, and in widening existing structures. Creative thinking occurs when the boundaries of the known are first mastered, through convergent processes, and then extended, by the application of divergent processes.

THE THRESHOLD ARGUMENT

Related to the view that creativity interacts with intelligence in producing a high level of achievement, by building on the more convergent kinds of processes as a base, is the notion that there may well be an IQ threshold below which divergent processes cannot operate, and above which they become independent. McClelland (1958, pp.12-13) is usually credited with having first introduced this threshold concept. He argued that there is a close relationship between IQ and achievement until some critical level is reached, after which level of achievement is no longer directly related to IQ but is determined by other factors. This notion has been extended to divergent thinking by Anderson (1960) with the suggestion that, after a cut-off point in IQ has been reached, effective creative functioning begins to depend on factors other than merely IQ. Thus, the threshold notion suggests that at lower IQ levels any creative achievement is largely limited by the level of IQ, but that, once some minimum IQ has been reached, creative abilities will be able to exercise themselves independently, if they are present. In this conception creativity would only really begin to affect achievement substantially if the minimum level of IQ had been surpassed, or to put it differently, divergent processes would only come powerfully into play if convergent processes had been sufficiently developed to permit appropriate mastery of the relevant field.

Torrance (1962a, p.63) proposes about 120 as the IQ threshold beyond which creativity bears a relationship to classroom performance which is independent of IQ. Yamamoto (1964c) investigated this point of view by selecting the top 20 per cent of students in a secondary school on creativity and then further dividing this group into three IQ groups consisting of those with IQs above 135, those between 120 and 135 and those with IQs less than 120. When the achievement of these three groups, on a large number of achievement measures including quantities like social sciences, natural sciences, general vocabulary and so on, was compared, he found marked evidence for a threshold effect. The two groups with IQ greater than 120 achieved much the same scores on the various measures, the middle IQ group sometimes surpassing the high IQ group, but the low IQ group (IQ less than 120) was surpassed by both other groups on every achievement measure.

Thus, despite the fact that there were no differences in creativity between the three groups, the students with IQs below 120 achieved well below the level of those above 120. On the other hand, once an IQ level of 120 had been reached, further increases in IQ made no differences as far as achievement was concerned. The present author's findings reported earlier in this chapter also support the notion of an IQ threshold. His two high IQ groups, like Yamamoto's, differed significantly on achievement when subdivided according to divergent thinking. Thus, at least beyond an IQ level of about 120, highly creative thinking adds importantly to school achievement.

Summary

A RECONCILIATION OF THE TWO POINTS OF VIEW

The two views discussed in this section: that creativity adds to achievement by building on to conventional intelligence; and that a minimal level of IQ is necessary for high levels of achievement, but that, beyond the minimal level (threshold) the presence or absence of creativity is determined by other factors (like, say, personality) are clearly reconcilable. The position basic to both points of view may be summarised in the generalisation that divergent thinking and convergent thinking interact in achievement. They are, in fact, not independent intellective modes which operate separately from each other, but interdependent facets of intellect, although the degree of interdependence decreases as IQ increases, and may reach zero at very high IQ levels.

INTERACTION WITH THE TEACHER

At this juncture, the present chapter may be closed appropriately by referring to a point raised by Yamamoto (1963), which stresses that there is, in fact, a fourth variable interacting with IQ and creativity, to lead to various levels of achievement. This extra variable is the teacher himself. In this study, he examined the effect of high teacher creativity and low teacher creativity on all members of grade five in a suburban school system in Minneapolis. He showed that, in the case of arithmetic skills, children of low creativity taught by low creative teachers did better than children of either middle or high creativity, after the effect of IQ differences had been removed. When teachers were highly creative thinkers, however, low creative students did worst of all. In the latter case, more creative students did better than did the uncreative children. Although he is cautious about making any generalisation on the basis of the data analysed in this study Yamamoto concludes that there is evidence that the relationship between creativity in students and their classroom achievement is partly dependent upon the levels of creativity in the teacher.[1] In particular, it should be noticed that children of low creativity easily surpass highly creative pupils when their teachers are themselves low on creativity. Thus, although there is a tendency for highly creative children to surpass highly convergent youngsters in academic achievement, this tendency which apparently becomes independent of IQ above about 120, is inhibited, or even reversed, when teaching is strongly convergent in nature.

[1] The role of the teacher in inhibiting or facilitating divergent thinking in pupils is discussed in greater detail in Chapter 6.

3

What Kind of People are Creative Thinkers?

Creative Thinking and Cognition

INTRODUCTION

The first two chapters all add up to the fact that there are capable people whose intellectual *modus operandi* differs from the one best suited to getting high scores on conventional intelligence tests. These people think in a divergent way and can be identified, nowadays, by their high scores on creativity tests, a kind of test which has only recently received much attention among educators.[1] Nevertheless, it is not correct to say that all divergent thinkers do badly on the convergent kind of test. In fact, the top 20 per cent of scorers on convergent tests usually includes about a third of those who are in the highest 20 per cent on creativity, and these people—high on both divergent and convergent thinking—seem to do particularly well in the classroom situation.

Nonetheless, there is still a large group of highly capable people who are likely to be labelled 'average' or even 'below average', not so much on the basis of low levels of intellectual ability, but rather because they tend to operate in a highly divergent way and get little chance to demonstrate their powers when they take an IQ test. The evidence for the claim that such people are wrongly labelled by IQ scores lies in the fact that people who get high scores on creativity tests often

[1] A more detailed discussion of tests of creativity is to be found in Appendix B.

do well on school achievement measures—some authors even assert that they do as well as children who score high on IQ tests, despite large IQ differences in favour of the latter group. Thus, if IQs alone are considered, there is a marked tendency for highly creative thinkers to be underestimated, a tendency which is particularly apparent in language subjects.

In short, then, there are some people who do well in the classroom on the basis of divergent rather than convergent thinking, despite the fact that, in many cases, their IQ scores would not lead to an expectation of such high levels of performance. The present chapter is concerned with the question of just what kind of people such creative thinkers are. How do they come to grips with the world? What kinds of personalities do they have? Do their personalities differ in some systematic way from those of convergent thinkers? Do they process information about the world in special ways? And so on. In fact, the chapter is concerned with an attempt to show that the disposition towards creativity is not simply a matter of intellect, but is closely linked with characteristic cognitive and personal qualities in an individual.

S-R PSYCHOLOGY AND COGNITIVE PSYCHOLOGY

It is common, nowadays, to draw a contrast between those psychologists who see psychological processes as essentially involving the building up of associations between stimuli and responses (S-R theorists), and those who are chiefly concerned with the ways in which people take in, organise, store, and eventually output information so that it can be readily retained and quickly retrieved (cognitive theorists). At the extreme the two kinds of psychology tend to concentrate on separate aspects of human functioning, the S-R theorists being concerned largely with learning in all its manifestations, cognitive theorists concentrating more on processes like thinking. However, the essential difference between the two points of view is not really one of different subject matter, but of differing approaches to the same phenomena. Thus, S-R psychologists are frequently also concerned with things like thinking, the nature of personality, the processes of forgetting, and so on, but they approach these topics in their own characteristic way. Similarly, cognitive psychologists may investigate learning phenomena. The difference between the two approaches to psychology lies, in fact, in the mechanisms they see as underlying psychological functioning, rather than in the subject areas they study.

Thus, S-R psychologists have attempted to account for the phenomena of creativity in their own way, which involves the notion that human behaviour is essentially a matter of building up links or bonds between stimuli and responses, although they are inclined to disagree among themselves concerning the mechanics of bond formation. In fact, within the general framework of the S-R approach, there are several theories of how creative thinking comes to occur: one or two of these will be outlined very briefly in the following paragraphs.

SOME S-R THEORIES OF CREATIVITY

Mednick (1962) has advanced a theory of creativity which is of the associative sort. He defines creativity as involving the formation of associations between stimuli and responses which are characterised by the fact that the elements linked together are not normally associated. Thus, he suggests that divergent people tend to link stimuli with highly unlikely responses, whereas in most people any particular stimulus is usually linked with the response with which it has most frequently been paired in the past. In other words, highly divergent people are particularly skilful at linking together, in an effective way, aspects of their environment which, on the basis of experience, do not really belong together. In most people, such happy S-R linkages seldom occur, except perhaps by chance,[1] whereas they are more or less commonplace among highly creative individuals.

[1] Hebb (1949, p.219) has suggested that the term 'serendipity' is now well established as a label for fortuitous, happy combinations.

THE REMOTE ASSOCIATIONS TEST

On the basis of this point of view, Mednick has designed a test of creativity. The Remote Associations Test (RAT), as he called it, assumes that highly creative individuals will make a greater number of associations to any given stimulus word than will less creative people. In each item of Mednick's test, subjects are presented with three words which have some common association, and they are required to find a fourth word which has common associative links with all three stimulus words. The RAT has been roughly standardised by Mednick and was reported by him to correlate with faculty ratings of the creativity of students in an architectural design course, and with ratings of research creativity of post-graduate students in psychology. It was also shown that high RAT scorers tended to be more 'liberal' in their views than low scorers, and that they expressed significantly more interest in creative occupations like journalism and art.

However, there is evidence, cited by the present author (Cropley, 1966), which suggests that the RAT is more related to conventional verbal skills than to divergent thinking, and that the associational theory of divergence is probably inadequate.

INSTRUMENTAL CONDITIONING AND DIVERGENT THINKING

It is also possible to formulate an S-R theory of creativity in terms of instrumental conditioning. Basically, instrumental conditioning involves the building up of S-R bonds by rewarding responses which are desired and failing to reward, or even punishing, linkages which are not required. Many authors have emphasised the role of such differential reinforcement in the building up of patterns of behaviour in children, and emphasise that their behaviour is shaped by the particular patterns of reinforcement received during the process of growing up. This point of view suggests that the extent to which a child is able to make creative responses will be heavily dependent on the extent to which he has been rewarded or punished for creative thinking during his past childhood, and implies that parents will have an important effect on the disposition towards creative thinking, as a result of their child-rearing practices. The possibility of such a relationship will be discussed in a later chapter.

OTHER S-R APPROACHES TO CREATIVITY

More recent S-R theories have placed great emphasis on the so-called 'mediating processes', and a number of complex formulations have been advanced which, while retaining their essentially S-R nature (by sticking to the idea that links between stimuli and responses are the basic units of human behaviour and even of higher-level intellectual processes), have proposed that there are various structures which intervene between the S-part and the R-part of the S-R bond. An example of one such formulation is that of Osgood (1953). However, all such attempts to account for the phenomena of creativity in terms of the S-R view ignore the individual himself as an important element in the connecting of environment and behaviour. The person becomes merely some kind of storage place which is at the mercy of the external world, and which is essentially passive. In fact, many psychologists reject such a view, and insist that the most interesting determinants of whether or not a person functions divergently or convergently lie, not in his conditioning history, but in his properties as a human being. Thus, in this conception, the individual is seen as actively engaged in the business of living, and creative thinking is linked to his personal properties, as well as to the power of his intellect.

THE COGNITIVE POSITION

Hence, in contrast to S-R theories of creativity, cognitive theorists are chiefly concerned with the ways in which people organise information received from the world. The individual is regarded as actively at grips with his environment, not merely the passive recipient of whatever it chances to offer him. Different people possess differing ways of 'taking hold of' the external world; they receive information in characteristic ways, interpret it idiosyncratically, and store it in terms of all the information processed in the past. Intellectual functioning is thus seen as a highly unified process so that the attempt to break it down into discrete fragments in the S-R way is bound to be inadequate. Hence, in accounting for the appearance or absence of creative thinking, cognitive psychologists are concerned with differences between highly creative and highly convergent individuals in the characteristic ways in which they come to grips with their environment.

Consequently, as far as cognitive theorists are concerned, creativity represents not differing systems of associational bonds, but different ways of getting and handling information, and different ways of combining data in seeking effective solutions (different 'mind styles' if you like). Hence, the cognitive approach to creativity asks about the extent to which highly creative people are prepared to take risks in their thinking, about their willingness to take in large quantities of the information the environment has to offer (rather than to restrict themselves to a narrow, but safe, segment of it), about their capacity for quickly changing their point of view, and so on. The remainder of this section will be concerned with a discussion of the relationship between high levels of creative thinking and several such cognitive variables.

CREATIVE THINKING AND DATA CODING

As Bruner (1957) has pointed out, any individual in contact with the external world is confronted with masses of data, too much, in fact, for him to handle. If he tries to take in everything, he suffers a good deal of 'cognitive strain' (Bruner, 1963, p.134). What happens is that individual environmental events are tied in with previous events so that new data are seen, not as unique occurrences, but as part of a related sequence of events which the environment has been providing throughout life. Thus, a new datum is rendered 'meaningful' by being connected with past data which it resembles. This process of connection is called 'coding', and a set of related data is called a 'category'. The point is that the external world is rendered meaningful by the linking of new events with past events which they resemble, and Bruner sees this as the chief kind of intellectual activity.

Now the contents of categories are built up through experience, so that, in members of the same culture, systems of categories tend to be highly similar. This in turn means that a given event will tend to be coded in a similar way by most members of a given culture—coding becomes highly stereotyped, in fact. Nonetheless, some people, despite their common cultural background, retain the capacity to make novel and unusual codings which manifest themselves as creative thinking.

Clearly, the more a person treats data which look to have nothing to do with each other as though they are related, the more likely he is to make data combinations which are unusual (i.e. to think creatively). The kind of person who codes in this broad way is referred to as a wide categoriser, while the opposite kind of person is called a narrow categoriser. People who make very fine discriminations between bits of input and who require high levels of similarity before they can see relationships (narrow categorisers), are inclined to store information as though it consisted of a large number of relatively unrelated, specific bits, and are thus unlikely to make the kind of cognitive leap involved in creative thinking. On the other hand, willingness to treat data whose connection with each other is not immediately apparent as roughly equivalent would be particularly favourable to the appearance of creativity. Creative thinking thus looks to be related to width of categorising.

In fact, this prediction of a relationship between width of coding and creativity, made on theoretical grounds, has been substantiated by empirical data. Wallach and Kogan (1965, p.129) sorted out a sample of 151 fifth grade American children into high and low creativity groups and also into high and low IQ groups, then obtained scores from them on a number of cognitive variables, of which category width in the sense outlined on this page was one. Analysis of the scores of the seventy boys and the eighty-one girls separately indicated that, in both groups, there was a significant tendency for the more highly creative children to get higher scores on the category width test.

This finding was supported by an analysis of category width scores obtained in the present author's own study with Canadian children. The 320 children were subdivided, on the basis of their scores on the creativity measures, and two special subgroups selected. These consisted of the top 10 per cent of the total sample on creativity, and the bottom 10 per cent on those measures. The highly creative 10 per cent of the children showed a marked tendency to get higher scores on category width than did the low creative 10 per cent. Thus, the empirical evidence supports the prediction made on theoretical grounds. Creative thinkers are, in fact, markedly broader in the width of their categories, so that they are able to see data equivalences which are not at all apparent to more convergent individuals.

CREATIVITY AND COGNITIVE STYLES

In the previous section it was stressed that intellectual functioning may usefully be thought of as involving the build up of codes, in which information about the recurring regularities of the world is stored. In this conception, the emphasis is on individual differences in the way in which data is stored once it has got into an individual's data processing systems. However, it is apparent that the presence or absence of creative thinking might well be connected with differences in the way in which environmental information is taken in, in the first place. Different people go about the matter of getting data from their environment in differing ways, so that, for example, some people concentrate closely on a small portion of what is available for input while others attend, in a less punctilious way, to a wider sweep of information. Such differences in the ways in which different individuals go about taking in the world are, in fact, so pervasive and so well documented that a label for the phenomenon is in widespread use among psychologists. The characteristic way in which an individual goes about taking in information from the world is referred to as 'cognitive style'. The cognitive styles whose existence have been demonstrated include 'field dependence', 'scanning-focusing', 'levelling-sharpening', and a number of others.

Most cognitive styles, including the ones just mentioned, have in common the property that they involve a dichotomy between, on the one hand, taking the world in in large lumps and, on the other, selectively attending only to chosen portions of the environment. The dichotomy can be restated as being a matter of paying attention to as wide a range of environmental properties as possible, or selecting a few attributes of the environment and concentrating on processing them. The latter strategy has the advantage that one can select a few highly related and task-relevant pieces of information and focus attention on them. This makes for ease of coding and necessitates little accommodation (modifying of codes), but that state of affairs is achieved at the expense of losing the capacity to make rapid changes in one's cognitive structures. In other words, the highly selective kind of cognitive styles lead to stereotopy of intellectual functioning, but have an important advantage in that they make life much easier.

On the other hand, taking in as much information as possible involves the risk of cognitive strain, necessitates frequent modification of existing categories, and makes intellectual functioning a more arduous task. However, this state of affairs leads to good pay-offs in that it involves the advantages of being able to change one's existing mental structures very readily, of being able to relate widely different looking data and, in fact, of being in a state highly favourable to the appearance of creative thinking. Thus, those people whose cognitive style involves the least censoring of the information available in the external world are most likely to be creative thinkers.

RISK TAKING

A cognitive variable which is closely related to category width, and also to cognitive styles involving readiness to accept the maximum amount of information from the external world, is that of risk taking. The convergent thinker has a pretty clear picture of just what goes with what. He knows what is logical, what not, and his world is a well organised and neat place in which he can expect to get along without too much strain. By contrast, the wide categoriser, who is prepared to attend to a broad variety of environmental information, must continually run the risk of making mistakes, or of looking foolish. He cannot rely on a set of well-worn tried and trusted principles to carry him through, but must adjust himself continuously to all available data. In this process, he may often be wrong, or certainly out of step with most of his fellows, so that he must risk making errors and being censured. Some authors, like McClelland (1963, p.184) and Roe (1963, p.170) for example, regard such willingness to take risks as so important in creativity that they mention it as one of the critical attributes of the highly creative individual.

Very closely linked with the notion that the creative thinker is not afraid to take a risk with his ideas is a further related trait—creative people are willing to 'have a go', intellectually speaking. They will, for example, risk an intelligent guess in a problem situation, whereas convergent thinkers are much more inclined to report that the problem is simply insoluble when it becomes apparent that logic, rule, and principle will not provide a solution. The latter kind of thinkers may even refuse to go on, on the grounds that the situation is 'foolish'.

The possibility of a relationship between creativity and risk taking was tested by a further analysis of the Canadian junior high school data already referred to in Chapter 2 and earlier in this chapter (Anderson and Cropley, 1966). The two sub-samples consisting of the most creative 10 per cent and the least creative 10 per cent of the entire 320 students were compared on a risk taking test, and the results indicated that the highly creative thinkers were significantly more willing to take intellectual risks by, for example, having a guess in a problem situation and then backing their own guess in the absence of any better information, rather than playing it safe by making a neutral estimate and expressing no confidence whatsoever in it. These findings are important because they strongly suggest that there are cognitive differences between creative and convergent thinkers, and further suggest that these differences are connected with the fact that the highly creative thinker is, to put it plainly, prepared to think boldly.

RIGIDITY

Thinking of the creative individual as a wide categoriser who attends to a broad span of environmetal events and is willing to take a chance on being wrong, of looking foolish, or of drastically having to revise his views, leads to a consideration of the role in creative thinking of rigidity and flexibility. The creative thinker is, above all, flexible and adaptable in his intellectual functioning. He is not committed to the preservation of an existing *status quo,* and is prepared to rearrange his thinking. On the other hand, the rigid individual is convinced of the logic and rightness of his existing view of the world. He is unwilling to make rapid or drastic changes in intellectual orientation, perhaps even incapable, and he clings firmly to what he 'knows' is right. In this latter kind of person, the intellectual flexibility which characterises the creative individual is missing, and he functions in a highly convergent manner.

This section may thus be summarised by saying that highly creative individuals are characterised, in the cognitive domain, by:

1 possession of wide categories;
2 willingness to take risks;
3 willingness to 'have a go';
4 high levels of flexibility.

Creativity and Personality

The variables discussed in relation to creativity in the previous section were connected with individual differences in techniques for coming into possession of environmental data, and in organising and storing information once it has been received. In this sense, they are not strictly aspects of personality, although closely linked with personality and frequently studied along with it. The following section is concerned chiefly with the relationship between certain traits which are more clearly traits of personality, and the presence or absence of creativity. The basic position adopted is that some personality organisations permit or foster creativity, while other organisations inhibit, or even preclude, it and so characterise individuals who function in the convergent way.

CREATIVITY AND PLAY

One characteristic of highly divergent individuals which has struck many observers, is their 'playfulness'. They may, for example, be particularly good at things like making up humorous story titles, as was the case with the highly creative high school students studied by Getzels and Jackson (1962). They often display a particularly lively sense of humour, and are frequently unusually alert to the funny side of life and especially good at making up humorous responses to tests. So marked is the preference for humour among highly divergent people that Weisberg and Springer (1961) described it as one of the best discriminators between the most divergent people whom they studied and the least divergent. Hudson too (1963) has commented on the significantly greater frequency of humorous responses among divergers than among convergers, and has linked this avoidance of humour among convergers to a general tendency on their part to 'compartmentalise' experience. In fact, Hudson has developed this point in a way which is highly relevant to remarks in the present chapter about the ability of divergent thinkers to code widely and their willingness to take risks. He suggested that the converger is a person who 'achieves a sense of security by restricting himself to a relatively narrow range of impersonal, technical topics' (1963, p.913). This view of the converger gets at both the ideas of narrow coding and of low risk taking which were suggested as important discriminators between divergent and convergent people, in the previous section of this chapter.

Creative people's playfulness may also manifest itself in the ability to 'play with' the meanings of words so that they see new aspects to them which have not previously been seen (Gordon, 1961). They may 'play' with the meanings of fundamental laws and principles and eventually arrive at unusual solutions to problems, or they may 'play' with common objects until they see implications which have not previously been noticed. What such play involves, essentially, is the capacity to look at the familiar in a new light, and to break the set imposed by the stereotypical meaning of any particular stimulus. Many creative people, among them Einstein (Gordon, 1961, p.41), have made this point about their own creativity, describing the way in which they play with ideas in seeking novel solutions.

PSYCHOANALYTIC FORMULATIONS CONNECTED WITH 'PLAY'

Psychoanalytic theory stresses the importance in creativity of the non-rational processes referred to as 'play'. Freud (1910) has argued that there are two main kinds of processes regulating ideas—primary processes and secondary processes. Primary processes are free of the restraints of logic, but secondary processes, on the other hand, are strictly rational and logical. What happens as an individual matures, is that he is increasingly obliged to depend on secondary process thinking, as he learns from his culture what goes with what, what is allowable, what not, and so on. Primary process thinking, which permits running in together of apparently quite separate ideas, toleration of apparent contradictions so that any ideas may coexist (regardless of how mutually exclusive they seem to be), and the formation of very loose connections between ideas, is firmly rejected by most people and thinking becomes highly logical, rational, and lawful. Creative thinkers, on the other hand, retain the capacity to admit primary process material into their thinking, which is thus considerably enriched by ideational linkages strictly repressed in the person completely dominated by secondary processes. A free intermingling of ideas normally kept discrete by the logic of secondary processes is possible, and out of this free fusion of ideas creativity arises.

More recent psychoanalytic theorising contends that the effect of the ego is to rigidify and inhibit idea-shuffling, so that creative thinking necessarily involves the relaxing of tight ego control of the flow of ideas. This relaxation, in turn, is only possible when the individual is confident of his ability to get back into ego control of the situation, so that highly creative people would be expected to display very strong egos.

While psychoanalytic theorising is, in most cases, no more than a very elaborate body of theory which has seldom been tested empirically and appears to be largely untestable, psychoanalytic theorists have made a very useful contribution to knowledge about creativity. In particular, they have forcefully drawn attention to the fact that certainly personality organisations seem unable to 'unbend' in a manner favourable to the creative processes. Further, they have emphasised, in the concept of ego-strength, that the capacity for creative thinking looks to be related to a kind of psychological 'secureness' which permits boldness in intellectual functioning.

CREATIVITY AND IMPULSE EXPRESSION

Basic to the psychoanalytic positions described in preceding paragraphs is the notion that some individuals tightly control their own impulses, while others are prepared to express them, and this dichotomy appears to be one of the basic personality differences from individual to individual. Luria (1961), for example, regards the very essence of development during childhood as centring around the learning of impulse control, and he suggests speech as the key factor in the achievement of control. In this conception, the developing child is seen as acquiring control of his own behaviour through the internalisation of adult verbalisations. The child learns, as it were, 'stop-rules' (Miller, Galanter and Pribram, 1960) which channel his behaviour into courses which reflect what the adults around him regard as 'right' behaviour. These adults in turn, are heavily influenced in their notions of rightness and wrongness by the culture in which they live, so that the general effect of the child's acquisition of control is that behaviour is kept within certain limits which are common to the whole culture.

Clearly, the child who controls his own thinking to the greatest degree will display the highest levels of stereotopy in his thinking and will be scarcely, if at all, capable of creative thinking. Conversely, creativity will be facilitated by a not-too-scrupulous adherence to the cultural rules of the game, and by the consequent retention of willingness to express impulses, even when the 'right' thing to do is to control them. This point is forcefully supported by the differences between Tom and Kathy as far as impulse expression was concerned. The highly creative Kathy was very ready to express impulses and emotions; the highly convergent Tom, on the other hand, kept his impulses strictly under control, except when they overwhelmed him.

Freud (1910) too has suggested that impulse expression is an important personality characteristic. During infancy strong pressures are brought to bear on a child to make him suppress natural urges and to express them only in the desirable way, and at the desirable time—for example, during toilet-training. Two outcomes of these pressures are possible: the child may internalise parental injunctions, thus acquiring the ability to control his own impulses in a socially approved way, or he may either fail to internalise the external edicts or even deliberately reject them. The first kind of child gets the payoff of social approval through a knowledge of the rules relevant to his culture, but this is achieved at the expense of impulse suppression. The second kind of child fails to learn the rules of the game (or perhaps, learns them, but refuses to be bound by them). His behaviour is thus likely to be nonconformist, original, and independent, but this is achieved at the expense of having to resist the culture's pressures to conform, and of the consequent probability of being censured for unconventionality.

DIVERGENT THINKING AND CONFORMITY

Reference to the nonconforming nature of the impulse-expressing type of person, in whom there is an increased probability of creative thinking, raises the whole matter of the relationship between creativity and nonconformity. To the extent that their divergent thinking is often accompanied by flamboyant nonconforming behaviour, creative thinkers frequently show up as highly unconventional types. In fact, however, the unconventionality is one of the concomitants of creative thinking, not creativity itself and, of course, mere unconventionality need not signal the presence of genuine creativity. Nevertheless, nonconformity is usually cited as one of the chief personality traits of creative thinkers.

Crutchfield (1955) has demonstrated a pervasive and stable dimension of individual differences centring around the fact that some people quickly revise their opinions when they are at odds with those of some larger group, even, in fact, when the group opinion is blatantly inaccurate but has been faked so that there appears to be consensus. Others, by contrast, stick to their guns when the evidence of their senses tells them that the group is in the wrong. Thus, faced with two lines of differing lengths, conforming individuals will agree that the obviously shorter of the two is really the longer, when they are confronted with a group of people who all agree that it looks longer to them, while nonconformers tend to resist the group's pressure to get their opinion into line. Such nonconforming individual's are marked, according to Crutchfield, by their willingness to express impulses and by their freedom from compulsion about rules, while conformers are marked by impulse suppression and strict attention to the rules.

Hence there is a good deal of evidence that an important aspect of individual differences in personality centres around the fact that some people control or overcontrol their own feelings and impulses, while others are much more willing to give expression to them. Furthermore, several authors have described other personality traits of those in whom levels of control are low, in terms which leave little doubt that these are the kind of people who tend to think creatively. According to Freudian theory, impulse expressing individuals are likely to be independent and nonconforming, and Crutchfield made a similar point. Barron (1955) has linked the less controlled personality directly to creativity by concluding that what he called 'orginality' represents a complex mode of responding to the environment, intimately related to personality organisations involving traits like rebelliousness, disorderliness, and independence of judgment.

In a later study, Barron (1963) showed that highly creative officers in the U.S. Air Force scored significantly higher on impulsivity than did their less creative colleagues. This tendency towards impulse expression remained significantly associated with high creativity even after the effects of intelligence were removed. From this evidence, Barron concluded that creativity is directly related to impulsiveness. Barron's linking of creativity with impulsivity has been supported by other empirical evidence too. For example, both MacKinnon (1962) and Garwood (1964) reported findings which showed that highly creative individuals tended to suppress their own impulses markedly less than did noncreatives. Tyson too (1966) has linked creativity to the kinds of personality traits discussed in this section, summarising the personality characteristics of the highly creative as involving 'independence, originality, "openness", intuitiveness, playfulness, and a sense of destiny'.[1]

However, probably the most convincing demonstration of the relationship between creativity and control is to be found in a point made by Hudson (1966). He pointed out that even highly convergent individuals can be got to behave in divergent ways by inviting them to pretend that they are artists or Bohemians, or by getting them under the influence of alcohol. In other words, convergent thinkers are capable of making responses of the divergent kind, it seems, if only they can be got to let themselves go.

All of this adds up to the fact that there are some people

[1] Tyson, M., 'Creativity' in Foss, B. M., *New horizons in psychology*. Pelican. P.178.

who keep themselves well under control, and regulate themselves carefully, in keeping with what is the culturally approved way of doing things. Conversely, there are other people who operate in a much bolder way—they are not afraid to give vent to their impulses, and do not keep themselves under such strict control. In view of the fact that several authors have reported evidence that this personality dimension of control is related to the appearance or non-appearance of creative thinking, some further data supplied by the 320 Canadian children already mentioned several times were analysed by the present author.

The two extreme groups on creativity were compared on a test of impulse expression and also on a test of the extent to which they concentrated on the private, idiosyncratic 'meanings' of stimuli in processing their environment, rather than on their public, objective meanings. Results indicated that the highly creative children were significantly more willing to give expression to their impulses and, further, that they displayed a markedly more pronounced preference for relying on the private associations elicited by stimuli than did the extremely low-creative group. This latter finding is supported by an identical conclusion reported by MacKinnon (1962) as a result of work done with highly creative architects. Thus, the present author's own research indicates that creativity and impulsivity are related.

Taken with the findings in the cognitive domain, the points made in the preceding paragraphs strongly suggest that there are major personality differences between highly creative and highly convergent individuals. The able converger, as compared with the able diverger, just will not relax control; he will not think boldly, and will not let go.

This difference between divergers and convergers is interesting in view of the suggestion made in Chapter 2 that creative thinking may become independent of IQ after a figure of about 120, becoming dependent thereafter on other factors, of which personality is one. The notions put forward in the present chapter support this view by indicating that there are certainly non-intellective determinants of whether or not a person will think creatively. Hence given adequate levels of intellect, it is very likely that personality is one of the chief factors determining whether thinking is likely to be of the convergent or divergent kind.

This view, in turn, has important implications in another area. If certain personality organisations are critical in determining whether a child will function creatively or noncreatively, it is apparent that those factors which are instrumental in shaping the developing personality will themselves be systematically related to the appearance of creative thinking. Thus it is likely that there are significant relationships between parental child-rearing practices and creativity. This point is developed in the next chapter.

4

Parental Training and Creativity

Relationships Between Child-rearing and Creativity

THE CULTURE'S DISAPPROVAL OF CREATIVE TRAITS

In the previous chapter, the creative child was described as essentially impulse-expressing and nonconformist. He tends to rely more on personal idiosyncratic 'meanings' of stimuli than on their objective properties, is prepared to guess, values play and humour as a legitimate form of idea-expression, and is prepared to take risks in seeking novel resolutions of data. He tends to be unwilling to accept authority blindly, is prepared to ask questions and is inquisitive. He is inclined to follow up something which has caught his interest, even if that involves working independently, and is thus sometimes seen as antisocial.

Paradoxically, despite recent lip service to the notion that creativity should be fostered, these qualities are precisely the ones which are usually regarded as undesirable in children. Torrance (1965a, p.230) has shown that in no less than five cultures which he investigated, including U.S.A., Germany, India, Greece and the Philippines, the cultures tended almost unanimously to disapprove strongly of properties like question asking, guessing, getting preoccupied with tasks, having the courage of one's convictions, disturbing classroom procedures, being emotionally sensitive, being independent in judgment and thinking, being intuitive in making associations, being willing to take risks, and finally, being unwilling to accept authority's say-so. On the other hand, all five cultures were almost unanimous in encouraging being willing to accept the judgment of authorities, being obedient, being industrious, getting work done on time, and being considerate of others. It is not the author's intention to suggest that there is anything wrong with being obedient, considerate and so on, but rather that there are dangers inherent in stressing possession of these highly desirable virtues as the *summum bonum* of child behaviour, and vigorously crushing any behaviours which seem to threaten the well-behaved, obedient, considerate passage of children through their childhood. Some authorities are not, in fact, worth accepting blindly, some established values could well do with a change, and there are possibly higher goods which even justify making someone else uncomfortable, or doubting the absolute rightness of the established order.

RELATEDNESS OF PARENTAL VALUES AND THOSE OF THEIR CHILDREN

It is usually accepted that the kinds of things that parents value, and their ideas about what constitutes desirable and what undesirable behaviour in children, tend to be reflected in the behaviour of the children. Although differing theorists describe in different ways the mechanisms by which parental and cultural ideas of what is right are transmitted, parents tend to pass on to their children a set of notions concerning 'right' and 'wrong' behaviour, and this set of notions tends to modify the ways in which the child is prepared to act. Furthermore, the views held by parents are culturally derived, and tend to reflect the value systems current within a culture. This state of affairs is particularly unfortunate where creativity is concerned, as the very behaviours which are necessary if creative productions are to result are severely frowned upon in most cultures, and are therefore not prized by conventional parents.

Hence creative children display behaviour and attitudes which are not popularly regarded as desirable within their culture.[1] It seems appropriate to wonder at this point, about the role of their home backgrounds in encouraging the appearance of high levels of creativity, despite the cultural bias against curiosity and the like. Do creative children tend to come from homes in which the parents' notions of right and wrong, of desirable and undesirable child behaviour, differ systematically from the ideas of the general populace? To put it plainly: Do highly creative children come from a special kind of home background which particularly facilitates the emergence of creative behaviour?

FAMILY BACKGROUNDS ASSOCIATED WITH HIGH CREATIVITY

Weisberg and Springer (1961), MacKinnon (1962), and Getzels and Jackson (1962), for example, have all suggested that the answer to this question is a definite 'Yes'. MacKinnon pointed out that he found, in the histories of a sample of highly creative architects, that certain aspects of their parents' attitudes to them as children were very important in providing them with the opportunity, and even the necessity, of developing qualities essential for creative performance in later life. Weisberg and Springer (1961, p.69) summed up this point of view neatly by referring to an 'optimal family pattern' which tended to maximise the likelihood of later divergent performance. Getzels and Jackson have made a similar point in describing the family life of three highly intelligent children, the Scotts, and comparing it with that of a highly creative brother and sister, the Blacks. Differences in the parent–child relationships are very striking and the tendency of high intelligence on the one hand and high creativity on the other to 'run in the family' suggests that there are special facilitating factors favourable to the two kinds of intellect in the two families.

The suggestion that highly creative children enjoy one type of relationship with their parents, highly intelligent another, may be put another way, by saying that one kind of parent–child interaction fosters intellectual functioning of the

[1] Hence the unconventional behaviour for which highly creative individuals are notorious.

divergent kind, while a different pattern of interaction fosters the convergent kind. This notion is supported by an examination of the child-rearing practices of Kathy's parents, and comparing it with the practices of Tom's mother. The differences are striking, and in the same direction as those reported by Getzels and Jackson. Hence it is argued that highly creative children are likely to have a characteristic kind of relationship with their parents, a relationship which fosters manifestation of their divergent thinking abilities. On the other hand, highly convergent thinkers tend to come from a markedly different background, as far as parental beliefs about 'correct' child-rearing practices are concerned.[1] It is appropriate to ask, at this stage, just what is the pattern of parent-child interaction which facilitates creativity.

Parental Practices Facilitating Creativity

A COMPARISON OF KATHY AND TOM

In Chapter 1, some details were given concerning the respective beliefs and practices of the parents of Kathy and Tom, highly creative and highly intelligent children. Some expansion of these details will be very useful in indicating a way in which parents of highly divergent thinkers differ from those of the highly convergent, as far as their interactions with their children are concerned. It has already been pointed out that Kathy's parents believed strongly in fostering egalitarianism and comradeship, while they were strongly opposed to fostering dependency and did not wish to break their daughter's will or be intrusive in their relationships with her. They were described, in round terms, as permissive and egalitarian. In fact, they expressed themselves as strongly in favour of statements like 'Children should be allowed to disagree with their

[1] It is not suggested that the kind of parental beliefs characterising homes which produce divergent thinking will necessarily guarantee that progeny achieve eminence as creative thinkers. Child-rearing practices will, nevertheless, facilitate the development of creativity where other determinants are present.

parents if they feel their own ideas are better', and 'Parents must earn the respect of their children by the way they act', while they were strongly opposed to statements like 'A young child should be protected from hearing about sex', and 'A good mother should shelter her child from life's little difficulties.' Thus, notions of over-protection are rejected (which does not necessarily mean deliberate over-exposure, as some people might suppose), and the child is encouraged to value his own opinions, where he can show that they are worth valuing.

In sharp contrast Tom's mother went to very great lengths to prevent him from doing anything 'foolish'. She did not permit him to make any decisions of his own, even about what he might do with his play time: play was given over to 'sensible' pursuits. He was taught always to look to external authority to guide him, and always to seek sensible and useful pursuits. Severe corporal punishment was used to see to it that he was quick to accept the edicts of authority and there was great emphasis on breaking his will (always, of course, 'for his own good'). Interaction between Tom and his mother was entirely devoid of any suggestion of cooperation—as the ultimate authority, her job was to issue authoritative edicts, his was to obey. (Incidentally, it should be pointed out, in passing, that Tom's mother was not a fiend, but a mother who passionately desired to see her boy successful and who was sparing neither her son nor herself in her determination that he should get on in life. In fact, he has 'got on' and is, no doubt, by her standards, a complete justification of her methods.)

Thus, Tom and Kathy's case histories suggest that the authoritarian, domineering, controlling parent who maintains a relatively cold and power-oriented relationship with children will tend to inhibit divergent thinking and foster convergent. Such parents intrude excessively into their children's lives, tending to limit the kinds of experiences which their children have and to censor the data they collect from the world. They emphasise hard work and logic as the answers to life's problems and are contemptuous of frivolity and play. The Getzels–Jackson case studies support this point of view.

THE SCOTT FAMILY

Getzels and Jackson (1962, pp.176-83) describe the Scott family in great detail, epitomising as they do the kind of home background particularly likely to foster thinking of the convergent kind. The Scott child who was closely studied was their daughter Lois, a nice, quiet girl who had an outstanding record throughout high school. She was particularly interested in maintaining high levels of classroom achievement, and suffered badly from nerves before examinations and tests. Nevertheless, taking her entire high school record into account, she was the most successful student in her school, although she was not quite at the top of any particular form. Her teachers enjoyed her hard work and enthusiasm, but felt that she had achieved these qualities at the expense of spontaneity and enjoyment of learning.

Lois's parents were well-educated and thoroughly pleasant people. Her mother was the acknowledged disciplinarian of the family, and she described her discipline as rigid but fair and consistent. Early in Lois's school life Mrs Scott had actually written to the school authorities complaining that too much time was being 'wasted' in efforts to foster the social development of the children, whereas she felt that they should concentrate on more serious matters. Mrs Scott emphasised in her general beliefs about life that working up to the highest possible standards of excellence is the main guiding principle that should be applied. She kept steady pressure on Lois to achieve well in school (compare her in this respect, with Tom's mother): the child was required to give a daily report on her school progress and her mother showed great interest in seeing that her daughter was always doing her best. The thing, even today, that makes Mrs Scott most proud of her daughter is that she is 'conscientious and effective'.

Mrs Scott described herself as having given a lot of thought to 'moulding Lois's life and character'. She was determinedly ambitious for her daughter. Lois, for her part, had internalised most of her mother's demands and, in particular, had adopted as her own, the mother's extremely high drive for 'success' in life as its main goal. Just before starting at university there was one moment when the high-pressure success orientiation might have been broken: Lois expressed a desire to leave school and get a job so that she could follow up her hobby of horse-riding—but the family soon got that kind of nonsense out of her head. By 1962 she was carving out a brilliant academic career at a first-class U.S. university, in the line which had been mapped out for her from the start.

The outstanding characteristics of the Scott household included heavy parental emphasis on success, parent–child interactions chiefly based on the imposition of parental views of what is right and best on the child, and little sympathy on the part of the parent for the child's own interests and wishes. The child had thoroughly absorbed the planned training to which she had been subjected from a very early age and, despite one or two minor rebellions which had been instantly crushed, had delighted her parents by the thoroughness with which she had lived up to their expectations. No doubt Lois will be applauded as an outstanding success throughout her life and, if she can handle the tensions and anxieties generated by her extreme achievement orientation, she will make a happy adult and mother, intent on raising her own children in just the same way as she was reared.

THE BLACK FAMILY

Like the Scotts, the Black parents are both well-educated people, and the father is a successful academic. Their son John was one of the Getzels–Jackson High-Creative group. However, Mrs Black lacked the poise and polish of Mrs Scott. She was rather untidy, but relaxed and friendly. The chief figure in their household was the father and, in fact, the household was organised around the task of meeting father's needs, rather than those of the children. Mrs Black had no special plans for the children and the central idea which dominated her behaviour towards them (which could be compared to Mrs Scott's desire to 'mould' her children) involved her desire to keep them healthy so that they could keep on functioning happily. Her relationships with her children were chiefly characterised by warmth and easiness and the thing which most pleased her about her children were their security and independence, whereas Mrs Scott, on the other hand, was most pleased by Lois's conscientiousness and effectiveness. The Black son, John, frequently disagrees with his parents on issues like his future career, although, in the main, they will be content to see him adopt any career which is likely to make him happy.

Father and son share many common interests, ranging from square-dancing and baseball-playing to watching 'egg-head' programmes on TV. Whenever the boy has developed a personal interest, or begun to worship a hero, the father has done anything he can to assist him. This includes such differing pieces of assistance as arranging a meeting with Dr Robert Oppenheimer and watching Mort Sahl together on TV. However, the father's role has chiefly been that of an assistant who brings his greater resources to bear on child-initiated activities.

In the case of the Blacks, it is apparent that the parents have adopted a quite different set of attitudes towards their children from those of the Scotts. They make little effort to control them, have no rigid long-range plans for them, permit them to make their own choices in the matter of things like interests and hobbies, warmly accept child opinions, and place little emphasis on being strictly right, sensible, successful, and so on. On the other hand, John is a very successful student and is regarded by his teachers as likely to go far in life, if he can control a certain erraticness of performance. In fact, then, both Lois Scott and John Black are high achievers and successful students. They both come from homes where, clearly, they have inherited high levels of ability, so that at birth both would have been good tips as babies likely to develop into highly successful adults.

However, the directions in which their potentials turned are diametrically opposite to each other. Lois's powers have developed to the high levels predictable from her heredity, but in a highly convergent way, while John, equally well endowed by nature, has developed along the divergent way. We are accustomed, nowadays, to the notion that heredity tends to impose upper limits on intellectual functioning by bequeathing to the infant a set of potentials, while environment is more concerned with regulating the extent to which potentials are realised, and the particular direction in which they develop. Consideration of the two families cited by Getzels and Jackson and of the case studies of Kathy and Tom suggest that one of the aspects of environment's guiding and directing functions may centre around its capacity to foster intellectual functioning which is predominantly divergent or convergent in nature. Of course, most people will probably be at neither extreme, since Lois Scott and Tom are obviously extremes both of convergence and of parental control, whereas John Black and Kathy are extreme in the other direction. Nonetheless, the evidence is that parents may greatly influence the kind of intellective mode preferred by their children.

A GENERALISATION

A number of authors have provided useful summaries of the outstanding characteristics of parents who produce highly creative children.

In his paper on creative American architects, MacKinnon (1962) pointed out that the architects' parents were remarkable in the extent to which they respected the opinions of their children and were confident in the children's ability to do what was appropriate in any particular situation. They allowed them to make decisions for themselves, even early in life, and behaved always as if they expected the children to act independently and yet still reasonably and responsibly: this kind of treatment was reflected, in the children, in an unusual sense of personal autonomy which underlay their high capacity for creative behaviour. Parents of the highly creative architects were, in fact, notable for their lack of intrusion into their children's intellectual privacy. An identical point has been made by Drevdahl (1964, p.175). He found 'striking differences' between creative and noncreative psychologists in the extent to which they had been given responsibility at early ages. The highly creative members of the group he studied came from home backgrounds where there was little coercion to produce 'right' behaviour. Like the parents of MacKinnon's architects, the creative psychologists' parents expected them to behave in a reasonable manner, but the expectation went unenforced. The children had personal responsibility for their own behaviour.

Weisberg and Springer (1961) found that parents of children who scored very high on tests like Tin Can Uses,[1] had parents who differed from those of low scorers in that the parents were highly expressive, but without dominating their children, and that they were also tolerant of regressive behaviour in their children. In other words, they did not frown upon immaturity, babyishness, illogicality and the like. Similarly, Stein (1963) found that creative research chemists had been more distant from their parents as children and had engaged in more solitary activity than had noncreative chemists. This finding supports the idea that lack of intrusiveness on the part of parents is important in the development in children of divergent patterns of thinking.

The kind of properties suggested as characterising parents of either children who score very high on divergent thinking tests or of scientists rated as creative in their particular discipline, have been linked to the kind of criteria normally associated with the word 'creativity' in its colloquial usage by Nichols and Holland (1963). They reported that literary achievement during first year university was significantly linked to non-authoritarian child-rearing attitudes on the part of parents of the students studied. Students who had made achievements in the literary field during first year by, for example, getting a poem or story published at least in a university newspaper, by having a play performed and so on, came from homes marked by high levels of parental tolerance for ambiguity and low levels of parental self-control. In a similar way, high levels of musical achievement were related to *laissez-faire* child-rearing practices in parents.

[1] See Appendix B for a description of this test.

Finally, Helson (1966) showed that the mothers of women who scored high on tests of imagination and artisticness were less nurturant (i.e., protective) and ambitious than those of low scoring women, while the fathers of the high scorers were more playful and argumentative, and less logical.

All of this may be summed up by saying that the kind of parents who tend to foster divergent thinking in their children are those who permit the child to function independently and treat him as a worthwhile person with worthwhile views of his own. The opposite kind of parent has his child's life carefully planned in advance, regards him as needing constant guidance (i.e., is vigilant), and brushes aside his wishes as mere foolish whims. The first kind of parents lay less stress on logic and order, and are thus sometimes inconsistent in their behaviour (Stein, 1963), but they are tolerant of playful, non-logical, regressive behaviours of the kind which are known to be important in creative functioning.

Cultural Norms and Sex Differences in Creativity

CULTURAL FACTORS DETERMINE ENCOURAGED AND PUNISHED BEHAVIOURS

The evidence, then, is that whatever levels of potential are present in a child, the direction in which they are developed (towards convergence or divergence), will be, at least partly, guided by the kinds of interactions the children have with their parents. In turn, the parents' thinking about how children should be treated is related to the way in which they themselves were reared and, in fact, to the prevailing cultural notions about what is right and what wrong behaviour in children. If a culture imposes severe negative sanctions against certain behaviours, most parents will try to suppress them in their children, while they will try to foster those behaviours of which the culture approves. Hence cultural norms act as a higher-level regulator of what behaviours parents rightly take into account in training their children since, whatever one's feelings about the validity of the sacred cows, it is much easier to get along in a culture when you are aware of where it dispenses its rewards, where its punishments.

The whole question of cultural standards and behaviour patterns is a very complex one, involving not only cross-cultural differences, but intra-cultural class differences, and so on, and it is not the present author's intention to develop these ideas fully here. However, one point of contact between cultural expectations and creativity, which is worth mentioning at this juncture, centres around the differing kinds of behaviours which are regarded as acceptable in girls as against boys.

BEHAVIOURS USEFUL IN CREATIVITY NOT PRIZED IN GIRLS

Consider the behavioural traits of the highly divergent person. He is likely to be adventurous, unorthodox, unwilling to accept authority, likely to ask awkward questions, humorous, and so on. These qualities may sometimes be valued in boys, in fact, out of the classroom are usually highly admired in boys, but they are seldom valued in girls. On the contrary, even in these days of emancipation, sex equality, and the like, the values accepted as characterising females, and most desirable in females, tend to be more concerned with meekness, being a lady (i.e., conforming), being well-behaved, working hard in school, and so on. Unorthodoxy is, even today, far more reprehensible in females than males, and the accepted behavioural norms for girls are considerably less favourable to divergent thinking than are those for boys.

Hence one would expect to find sex differences in creativity, and just such differences have been reported by various authors. Not only is it a fact of history that creative achievements in the past have been almost confined to males, but it has been demonstrated, for example, that girls tend to be narrower categorisers than boys (Pettigrew, 1958; Wallach and Caron, 1959). The present author too has shown (Cropley, 1965) that originality is a much better differentiated aspect of intellect in boys than in girls. In his study of Canadian junior high school children, teenage boys possessed more clear cut creative abilities than did teenage girls, and made use of them in divergent thinking problems.

However, it would be wrong to attribute these sex differences in creativity to basic inferiority of females in divergent thinking. As has been demonstrated earlier in this chapter, whether or not intellectual functioning tends to be mainly of the divergent sort, or mainly of the convergent, depends partly on the training which children receive from their parents. Hence if those qualities which are usually associated with the disposition towards creativity are almost universally frowned on in girls, it is scarcely surprising that few of them manage to develop into divergent thinkers. Thus, sex differences in creative behaviour are more likely to result from the differing cultural values applied to boys' and girls' behaviour than from innate female inferiority.

A Reconsideration

DANGER OF OVER-SIMPLIFICATION

The chief point made in the present chapter, up to this stage, can be briefly stated in the following way: parents who are permissive foster preference for the divergent mode of thinking in their children, those who are intrusive and viligant foster preference for the convergent mode. However, this generalisation, while a useful one, may well represent an over-simplification of the situation. In the first place, as might be expected from the discussion in the previous section of this chapter, boys and girls are differentially affected by traits like dominance in their parents, and are also differentially affected by the matter of whether the male or female parent is the one displaying the trait. The generalisation offered in the present chapter must thus be couched in the broadest terms if it is to be useful in summarising the situation for children of both sexes.

There is, however, a more serious deficiency in the idea that treating children one way makes them divergent thinkers, treating them in another makes them convergers. In an earlier chapter, it was stressed that children at school must be free to function in as varied and free a way as possible, and that they should not be forced into the convergent mode, since this represents a restriction on the scope of their intellectual functioning. However, forcing them into a one-sidedly divergent thinking style is equally undesirable, since functioning of the Low-High kind is as restricted as that of the High-Low style. If one is really interested in helping children to think in the freest possible way, it is thinking of the High-High type which should be fostered.

The generalisation is quite satisfactory in accounting for children who have a marked preference for the divergent mode at the expense of the convergent (Low-Highs), and is also adequate to account for those in whom the preference for the convergent mode is predominant (High-Lows). But it does not account for the existence of the two other groups consisting respectively of High-Highs and Low-Lows. If one kind of home background makes a child function in a divergent way and another makes him function in a convergent way, how is it that some people perform badly in both modes, while others do extremely well in both?

The Low-Low group can be accounted for relatively simply, by advancing the plausible argument that they are the people who lack the intellectual equipment to get high scores on abilities tests, regardless of whether the tests are designed to elicit convergent or divergent thinking. They are the non-able portion of the population, whose thinking is likely to be poor regardless of what mode is fostered by their home background. This point of view implies that the Low-Low group should be the largest of all four when children are selected from the population as a whole, since it contains all those who are in the lower segment of the population as far as intellect is concerned: this expectation has certainly been borne out in the present author's own research (e.g., Cropley, 1967). Pursuing the line of reasoning introduced in this paragraph would suggest that there are three groups of intellectually able people: those with a marked preference for the convergent style (High-Lows), those with a marked preference for the divergent style (Low-Highs), and those who can function with equal ease in either mode (High-Highs). The generalisation about home background and style of thinking accounts adequately for the existence of the first two groups, but cannot account for the third. If an able child can go either way, according to home background, how do some children come to be allrounders?

NEGATIVE PROPERTIES OF PERMISSIVE HOMES

This point of view, which says, in effect, that homes which produce children who get high scores on divergent thinking tests but do badly on convergent thinking tests are just as restrictive as those which foster the opposite kind of intellectual functioning, runs counter to most opinions expressed elsewhere, and looks as though it is inconsistent with remarks earlier in the present chapter. It is customary in the relevant literature to describe the qualities of the divergence-producing home in such a way as to imply a value judgment that this is a 'better' kind of parent–child relationship. In keeping with this notion the present author has presented only the positive and admirable properties of such homes, and has stressed that parents in them tend to respect their children's privacy, to value their opinions, and so on. However, research in the area has revealed a number of other properties of some of the homes which foster an extreme preference for divergence in children.

Thus Helson (1966) has pointed out that the mothers of high scorers on tests of imagination and artistic tendency described themselves more frequently as 'irritable' and 'touchy' than did mothers of low scorers, while their fathers described themselves less frequently as 'affectionate' and 'responsive'. Drevdahl (1964, p.179) reported 'an apparent element of emotional coolness' in the family relationships of many highly divergent thinkers, and Stein (1963, p.226) observed that highly creative research chemists were often 'more distant from either parent' than were less creative scientists. In fact, it is not uncommon to find references in the relevant literature which suggest that extremely divergent thinkers do not come from homes where all is sweetness and light, although there is a great temptation to those who are eager to see divergent thinking recognised as a desirable aspect of intellectual functioning to present their findings in such a way as to give this impression. Weisberg and Springer (1961, p.563), for example, observed that outbursts of hostility were likely in the homes of their highly divergent children and concluded that the home yielding highly divergent thinkers is likely to involve 'a chronically anxiety-provoking situation'.

The view which the present author would like to stress is that, while over-controlling parents who are ever vigilant of their children frequently produce children (and later adults, of course) who prefer the convergent kind of thinking so strongly that they may be almost unable to function in a divergent situation, grossly under-controlling parents whose contacts with their children are so permissive as to constitute almost aloofness are equally likely to raise youngsters whose preference for the divergent mode makes convergent functioning difficult, even in situations where some convergent activity is appropriate. (An example of such a situation would occur whenever a corpus of factual material needs to be mastered before divergent productions can commence.) Hence child-rearing practices which are markedly towards either extreme inhibit the development of the kind of people who are most versatile—the High-Highs, who can operate in either mode, according to the demands of a particular situation.

To say that a capable child is likely to develop along the all-round path when his parents' child-rearing practices are at neither extreme looks a little like begging the question, but the middle line, in this case, is not quite as simple a matter as it looks. What is needed is that parents give their children ample opportunities to function independently, and so on, but without this reaching the point of remoteness. Vigilance on the part of the parents is needed, but it must be practised unobtrusively, so that it does not reach the point of becoming intrusiveness. The kind of thing which can be done is discussed in Chapter 6, where the problem of maintaining contact, without instituting rigid control, is discussed in relation to the teacher in the classroom.

This section can be closed by saying that in an able person divergence unaccompanied by the capacity to function convergently represents intellectual inflexibility in just the same way as does convergence unaccompanied by the capacity for divergent thinking. Although over-control on the part of parents is clearly inimical to the appearance of divergent patterns of thinking in their children, a total absence of the kind of contacts involved in parental guidance, while fostering divergent modes of thinking, is in danger of producing people who are, in their own way, as one-sided as the rigidly convergent. What is needed is some kind of middle path.

5

The Creative Child and his Teachers

How do Teachers React to Creative Children?

AN EXAMPLE

An anecdote, describing an exchange between a child in a Canadian elementary school and his teacher makes a good beginning for this chapter. The author can vouch for the truth of the story. A grade one class had been told to draw a human head as an exercise during a drawing lesson, and had been quietly at work for some time when one member of the class left his desk, at which he had been working hard for several minutes, and came out to the teacher's table. The main purpose of the exercise had been to keep the class quiet for a while, so that the teacher could catch up on some paper work, and so she was not at all pleased to be disturbed by the particular student concerned. As a matter of fact, he was regularly inclined to make a nuisance of himself in this way. Consequently it was with some impatience that the teacher asked the boy what he wanted and why he was not at his desk working as industriously as the other members of the class.

The trouble was that the child had a problem on which he wished to consult the teacher, and the problem was revealed in the question he asked: 'Please Miss, do we have to draw the *inside* or the *outside* of the head?' He showed his partly completed drawing to the teacher—it consisted of a sketch of the inside of a human head, as the child thought it might look if the observer got inside somehow and looked around him! The teacher dismissed the child angrily, telling him to stop being such a fool and to get to work on a 'proper' drawing the same as all the other, more 'sensible', children were doing. She was sick and tired of his continual 'stupid' suggestions and 'ridiculous' questions. Everyone else had known what she meant, but he had had to be a fool and try to draw the inside of a head.

For those who have actually done some teaching, it is very easy to sympathise with the teacher concerned, especially as she had an over-large class and far too much form-filling to do. However, consider the effect on the child. For the tenth or twentieth time since he had begun school a few months before, he had made what seemed a good suggestion, or had asked what seemed a fair question, all in good faith. The response had been surprising and devastating—he had been labelled a nuisance, a loafer, and a trouble-maker. Such a child is likely to have the experience repeated as he progresses through the school system, the frequency of occurrence diminishing until eventually he learns to do the 'sensible' thing which everyone else does, and to stop being 'cheeky' to his teachers.

However, if one thinks about his question in the incident just described it is impossible to conclude that the child's behaviour had been wicked or even stupid. Just what is wrong with wondering what a person's head looks like from the inside? Why shouldn't he try to draw this unusual view of a head? The real reason for the teacher's anger was, of course, that he had threatened to produce some work which was not uniform with that of the rest of the class and so to disrupt the smooth flow of class activity. Especially if he is encouraged to make more and more divergent productions, such a child begins to make the teacher's job more and more demanding and to make it increasingly impossible to run the class in a routine way. Even in the class of a conscientious and hard-working teacher, a single such child can multiply the difficulty of running an effective and efficient classroom several times over. Furthermore, in a few years, he may easily begin to produce ideas which are beyond the capacity of his teachers to evaluate at all, and to ask questions which they cannot answer.

TEACHERS' PREFERENCE FOR NON-CREATIVE STUDENTS

Getzels and Jackson (1962, pp.30-3) have reported the results of a study in which teachers were asked to comment on the work of two groups of students, one group consisting of highly intelligent but non-creative students, the other of students who were 'highly creative' but relatively less intelligent than the first group. Their results showed that the teachers much preferred teaching the high IQ group to the high creativity group, a result which is particularly revealing when it is borne in mind that there were no differences between the two groups on academic achievement. In other words, the desirability of the students was not decided merely by classroom performance on academic work since the two groups were equal on this dimension. On the contrary, the teachers tended to discriminate between the two kinds of children, preferring the students whose results were obtained by the application of convergent, authority-centred, conventional thought processes over those who tended to be highly creative in obtaining equally good results.

This finding has been supported by Torrance. In a series of studies (Torrance, 1959) he was led to conclude that high IQ (as against high creative) students tended to be both better known and better liked by their teachers. Holland (1959) too has warned against placing much reliance on teachers' ratings of the creativity of their students, as they tend to downgrade the capacities of highly creative children with whom they come into contact, and actually to rate the preferred high IQ/*low* creativity children as more creative, presumably as a result of a pronounced halo effect. In fact, reviewing a text by Goertzel and Goertzel (1962), in which they examined the histories of a large number of children who grew up to become eminent adults, Torrance (1966) pointed out that many of the individuals whose histories were examined by those two authors were unhappy at school and found themselves suffering a great deal of 'psychological discomfort' as a result of the hostility of their teachers to their 'differentness'. He then went on to suggest that in many cases what the teacher really seems to desire in his pupils is conformity and blind reproduction of presented material.

Torrance has further pointed out (Torrance, 1965b; 1966) that teachers may even go as far as to describe highly creative children as mentally retarded. Many of the eminent persons studied by Goertzel and Goertzel (1962) were regarded by their teachers as defectives, while Torrance himself (1965b, pp. 51-2) cites a case from his files of a boy who had been regarded as gifted by his parents and pediatrician prior to his entrance to kindergarten, but who was regarded by his teacher as more or less mentally retarded. He was inclined, for example, to make additions to stencilled test papers distributed by his teacher, or to modify the material even more radically and to respond then, one supposes, in terms of the modified material rather than the original. He was consistently given failing marks in tests and, in this case, imaginativeness and nonconformity were regarded as signs of mental retardation. Although examinations by outside agencies consistently indicated that the boy was of above average intelligence, he continued to be regarded as a retarded child for several years—after some years of such treatment, it would scarcely be surprising if the child actually began to think of himself as a mental defective.

CONFUSION OF CREATIVE BEHAVIOUR AND MISBEHAVIOUR

One might well ask oneself, at this juncture, why teachers should be annoyed by creative behaviour in their students. In fact, one must bear in mind that it is extremely difficult to distinguish between truly creative behaviour and mere misbehaviour. There is a grave danger that the creative child will be lumped in with the mere unenlightened trouble-maker, especially when the end result of the creative behaviour is identical as far as the teacher is concerned, and involves interruption to the smooth flow of lessons, independence of thinking which looks suspiciously like unruliness, and individuality which begins to shade into rebelliousness.[1]

Creative students are often hard to get on with. They tend to endorse different value systems from their more conventional classmates and to have a different image of the world from most schoolchildren (and from most teachers too). Their questioning attitudes look very much like hostility and their liking for humour and wit is difficult to distinguish from mere 'smart' and puerile wisecracking, unless the teacher can see the line of thought underlying it. Often, honest curiosity, genuine independence of thought, and a pleasing wit, are taken by the teacher to represent rebelliousness and lack of cooperation which are thought to spring, not from divergence of thought processes, but from sheer malice.

The creative student poses a number of problems for his teachers and several of these—based largely on Torrance (1964, p.92)—are discussed in the following section.

Problems which the Creative Child Poses for his Teachers

THREAT TO DISCIPLINE

If it is difficult for a teacher to discriminate between misbehaviour and genuine creative behaviour, it is even more difficult for other members of the class. They may, for example, be hostile towards the creative child and frequently regard him as a trouble-maker and an outcast, although this is by no means always the case. Nevertheless, it is not at all uncommon for the teacher to find that the divergent activities of a child in his class are provoking a difficult situation by threatening a breakdown in class discipline. Not only is the teacher who is not conscious of the existence of creativity, and

[1] Once again, it should be understood that the author is not proposing that rebelliousness and unruliness always indicate the existence of previously unrecognised creativity and that they should, therefore, be prized in schoolchildren. What is being suggested is that behaviour which looks as though it springs from sheer wickedness is sometimes a reflection of genuine divergent thinking. The teacher's job is to make the appropriate distinction, encouraging the creative behaviour and quelling the other.

who values convergence and conformity above all else, likely to interpret divergent behaviour as misbehaviour and a threat to the maintenance of order, but even when the teacher is creativity-oriented, it is still often necessary to inhibit creative behaviour. This situation arises because the merely idle and malicious members of a class are likely to take advantage of any disruption of classroom procedure occasioned by the creative child, in order to indulge their own rebelliousness and unruliness. Hence divergent behaviour of the kind which creative schoolchildren often display presents a threat to discipline in two ways, even when it is recognised by the teacher for what it is: (1) It may be interpreted by the other children as nothing more than misbehaviour, so that the teacher who permits it seems to be weak or to be playing favourites; (2) it may provide an opportunity for genuine unruliness among other members of the class by disrupting the normal flow of classroom events.

In these circumstances by far the simplest solution for the teacher is to impose sanctions against divergent behaviour and to crush it severely. Even when the teacher can see that there is more than mere cantankerousness behind the behaviour, he can justify stern repression of it on the grounds that the greatest good (i.e., the maintenance of an orderly and effective classroom) takes precedence over the needs of one or two unusual children. The less well informed teacher might put it differently and say that the creative children need to learn that they can not go against the way the majority do things, or that it is high time they learned to be like everybody else instead of going off in queer ways, if they want to get along in life. In fact, if the treatment that many highly creative individuals receive at the hands of their peer groups is taken into account, it is difficult to maintain the view that this latter point is completely invalid.

UNEXPECTED RESPONSES

Another of the difficulties associated with the presence of highly creative children in the classroom centres around their disconcerting knack of producing highly unusual responses and completely unexpected solutions if they are encouraged to give free rein to their creative powers. The teacher may find himself badly disconcerted and even deflated by an apparently irrelevant, completely unexpected answer, at some vital point in a lesson which he has been carefully developing perhaps for half an hour or more. Especially when the child's suggestion is an obscure attempt at humour, or an apparent total irrelevancy, the effect can be quite devastating and can even take much of the point out of a well planned and well presented lesson.

The present author has had this experience on a number of occasions like, for instance, the time when, in a first form science lesson, he had been demonstrating that liquids expand when heated and contract when cooled. Having gone through the theory with meticulous care, he felt that the time for a practical demonstration had arrived. A flask had been filled with coloured water, a stopper and tube inserted, and the heat was about to be applied. Before beginning to heat the water, the class was invited to guess what would happen, on the basis of the theory which they had just had outlined to them. Eager hands shot up, the whole class's attention had been captured, and the stage was set for a really convincing demonstration. One eager student was selected to answer and the rest of the class groaned in disappointment that they were going to miss the chance to show what they could do by predicting that the liquid would expand and rise up the tube. Then came the answer: 'Please sir, what if the gas flame suddenly began to burn cold, instead of hot?' (The teacher had been talking casually some days before about gases which burnt at low temperatures and therefore gave off 'cold' flames.)

Of course, the rest of the class hooted in derision and the lesson threatened to be ruined if the teacher succumbed to the temptation to lecture the boy: 'You stupid child. How many times do I have to tell you . . .'. In this particular case, the day was partly saved by taking the question seriously and following it up in something like the following way: 'Very well, just suppose for a minute that the flame were actually cold instead of hot. What would happen?' The answer that the water level in the tubing would drop instead of rise was obtained and the lesson continued. However, it does not always work out so well, and there is no doubt that teachers are often disconcerted when they receive unusual responses where prosaic ones were anticipated.

DIVERSIONS WASTE VALUABLE TIME

Closely linked with the previous point is another which causes concern to many teachers. Especially in classes which have external examinations to face in the near future, there is usually little time to spare for frivolity. Frequently the teacher, even when he is conscious of the need to foster creativity, is tempted to tell the child what is 'best', in order to avoid wasting time. This need to save time becomes more and more pressing as the child advances through school and is possibly a valid aim on the part of teachers harassed by the need to get their children through difficult and vitally important examinations. In particular, it seems hard on the non-creative majority of a class that the flow of 'logic' and 'common sense' should be interrupted to satisfy possibly a single class-member.

EMBARRASSING QUESTIONS

When they are encouraged to give free rein to their creative tendencies, children are frequently inclined to embarrass their teachers by perceiving relationships which are not apparent to the teacher, sometimes which do not become apparent even after lengthy explanation on the part of the child. At senior levels, the creative child may actually become aware of significances which are not apparent, even to experts in the field, without careful examination of the issues involved. Coupled with this embarrassing habit is the tendency of the highly creative child to ask questions which his teachers cannot answer.

SANCTIONS AGAINST GUESSING AND PLAYFULNESS

An important aspect of creative behaviour involves the willingness of the highly creative child to speculate and guess. Such children may get a great deal of satisfaction out of making a bold guess which comes somewhere near the truth. However, most teachers have been schooled to look for solutions through the application of logical rules, and they tend to feel guilty about encouraging guessing. It is taken as self-evidently true in our school system that guessing is an inferior level of problem-solving activity, and the teacher who fails to eliminate guessing in his students may feel that he is doing them a grave disservice. For this reason, the guessing of the creative child is likely to be frowned upon by his teacher, and he is likely to be thought of as something of a nuisance.

As usual, the feeling that guessing is not a desirable problem-solving strategy is by no means a completely false notion. Uninhibited wild guessing is undoubtedly a maladaptive approach to a problem, and is unlikely consistently to lead to satisfactory solutions. In the case of the uninformed guess, any satisfactory solution reached is likely to occur merely as a happy accident. What the teacher must try to do is distinguish between the uninformed shot in the dark which is likely to lead nowhere, and the bold, imaginative guess, which may well short circuit the long and tedious processes of strict logic and lead to hitherto unseen solutions.

In a similar way, teachers have come to regard the classroom as an essentially serious place where frivolity and lightheartedness can only inhibit satisfactory progress. On the other hand, as has been pointed out in an earlier chapter, one of the characteristics of the creative child is his playfulness and his interest in wit and humour. Consequently he often annoys his teachers, especially when the point of his witticisms is not apparent to the teacher. This situation is aggravated by the fact that puerile wisecracking is one of the tactics frequently adopted by the rebellious, insolent trouble-maker whose 'humour' springs not from creativity, but from a desire to disrupt and destroy. The same point can be reiterated here as has been made in several other places—the teacher is faced with the difficult task of distinguishing between the two kinds of student.

Summary

The basic point made in this chapter is that teachers seldom enjoy having creative children in their classes, and tend to have strong preferences for the more orthodox, easily understandable children, of high IQ but low creativity. This is scarcely surprising when it is remembered that the creative student is often obnoxious, while the merely bright child, whose main aim in school is to satisfy the teacher's conventional expectations, warms the teacher's heart with his docility and earnestness.

The reasons for this lack of teacher regard for highly creative students were then considered in some detail and may be summarised by saying that the creative child is very frequently, to put it plainly, a nuisance. He tends to see the world differently from his teachers, he has different ideas of what are valuable and desirable ends, and frequently embarrasses his teachers, even when his intentions are good. When they are bad (and creative children are still children, after all, and perfectly capable of bad intentions), he has the advantage that he may often be quicker witted than his teacher, and more inventive in thinking up misbehaviours than is the teacher in combatting them.

The situation is further complicated by the fact that creative behaviours often look very much like sheer bloody-mindedness, so that teachers who are authority-orientated rather than creativity-orientated may interpret manifestations of creative thinking quite wrongly. Furthermore, even if the teacher is good at distinguishing true independence of thought from rebelliousness, a creative child who is encouraged can pose a number of problems of discipline and classroom control which make the teacher's job even more difficult than it is in any case.

Small wonder, then, that many teachers take the easy way out and treat all divergent behaviour as a threat and a nuisance, imposing severe sanctions against it. Even the well-informed teacher who wishes to foster creativity in his classroom must be continually alert, and always ready to think quickly if he is to perform effectively. The following chapter is concerned with the question of why teachers should seek to foster creativity, and how they can go about doing this.

6

Teaching to Foster Creativity

Why Encourage Creativity?

CREATIVITY IS IMPORTANT IN ITSELF

In Chapter 1 it was pointed out that the pressing need for more and more knowledge in the modern world, and the pressure on modern nations to utilise the intellectual potentials of their citizens to the maximum possible degree, make it essential for teachers to be aware of the distinction between intelligence in the IQ test sense and creativity. Creative skills are of vital importance these days and it is extremely important that teachers encourage their development to the fullest possible degree.

It has long been recognised that learning at the infant level can make effective use of the tendency of young children to be curious and to seek new situations. Infant teachers are well aware of the fresh curiosity of the school beginner and his willingness to seek challenges to his new-found skills. They are perfectly familiar (sometimes to their chagrin) with his tendency to raise problems and to ask illogical questions, along with his ability to visualise extensions of given situations which are 'logically' impossible. At this stage in the development of knowledge about creativity, it is relevant to ask whether the same attitudes might not be utilised in fostering the learning of more senior students. They need, in fact, not merely to be encouraged to test the improbable and unusual, but to be shown that dealing with the unknown and questioning the safely known are permissible, even desirable classroom activities. The realisation that talent is not completely confined to the possession of a high IQ logically implies that it is high time that teachers began to make use of creative skills at all levels of the educational process. Thus, creativity should be fostered in the classroom, in the first place, for its own sake, since modern education should aim at making it possible for every child to function in a free, bold and flexible way.

NOT ONLY THE HIGHLY CREATIVE ARE INVOLVED

At this point it should be made clear that the present author is not suggesting that every student in every classroom should be treated as though he is destined to become a creative genius of the Einstein or Shakespeare variety. On the other hand, it must not be supposed that a school curriculum which aims at utilising students' creative abilities will be lost on all but creative children. All children are capable of asking and wondering, of guessing and supposing, of questioning and speculating, so that a curriculum which fosters creativity facilitates learning in all students. In the case of the student with marked creative potential a creativity-centred classroom will help him to develop his creative talents to the full while, in the case of the non-creative, approaching knowledge through creativity will help him to understand the way in which knowledge is organised, and will make him a more efficient finder of adaptive solutions.

CREATIVE LEARNING IS INTRINSICALLY MOTIVATED

There are, however, good practical reasons for the classroom teacher to be concerned with creativity, for a creative approach to teaching goes a long way towards meeting one of the continuing difficulties which teachers encounter in their work. Material which is acquired by rote rather than by understanding has no built-in power to make the student seek more and more information. He may work very hard indeed at the task of acquiring facts, but the drive always comes from outside the knowledge itself, and involves things like success in examination, scholarship-winning, avoidance of parent and teacher disapproval and the like. There is nothing wrong with being successful in exams, of course, and the winning of scholarships is highly desirable and commendable, but learning which is aimed solely at these ends often has a sterility and a dullness which make it a meaningless process in itself. And furthermore, where such goals are not particularly prized by the child, the pursuit of knowledge is in danger of coming to a halt. On the other hand, material which is learned because it is in itself satisfying to the student's curiosity and ingenuity, and which is seen as a challenge to the learner's mental agility, needs no external rewards and punishments to keep the learning process in motion. Such material is said to be intrinsically motivated. That is to say, the getting of knowledge becomes rewarding in itself and the process goes on independently of external considerations.

CREATIVE LEARNING IS MORE EFFICIENT

Furthermore, knowledge has accumulated with increasing speed in recent years and the process of accumulation has begun to accelerate at a faster and faster rate, until teachers and students are faced with an ever larger and ever untidier mass of material which must be mastered. Individual subject areas have become increasingly specialised, necessary background material becomes more voluminous, and the contents of merely a 'basic education' become ever more extensive. In the face of this logarithmic growth, it is critically important that the knowledge-getting skills of children should neglect no mechanism which facilitates learning. Mere rote methods are no longer adequate to the task of effective learning. New approaches to the fostering of effective learning are required, and it is increasingly being suggested that creative thinking abilities can contribute significantly to the acquisition of knowledge when they are appropriately utilised. The point is that, in a changing world, all the potentials of a child's intellect should be brought to bear on the process of interacting with the environment, not just one aspect of them.

This view has been advanced by Getzels and Jackson (1962) and by Torrance (1964). The latter author has suggested that knowledge of the fact that human beings learn best when they learn creatively is by no means new, but that it has been more convenient for teachers to employ authoritarian methods in their classrooms. An authoritarian approach is certainly easier on the teacher, involving him in less preparation and relieving him of the necessity to be at his peak of classroom performance at all times. However, as the experiments of Moore (1961) and Ornstein (1961) among others, have shown, creative learning is more economical than mere rote learning, and it is even true to say that some children who learn poorly by conventional methods are effective learners when their teachers utilise their creative thinking abilities. Thus, the plain fact of the matter is that *teaching techniques which utilise students' creative thinking abilities promote more effective and efficient learning than those methods which ignore them.*

Can Creative Learning be Taught?

THE QUESTION

Having pointed out that there is a growing need for an extension of traditional classroom methods so that they utilise the child's inquiring, inventive capacities (his creative abilities), it is appropriate to ask whether creativity can be taught; and just what this would involve for the school teacher. This section and the one which follows will be concerned with looking at the evidence which suggests that it *is* possible to foster creative thinking and learning by appropriate classroom procedures, and with outlining some ways in which the teacher can achieve this end.

Attempts to teach creativity formally as a subject in the school curriculum are unlikely to meet with much success. In the first place, the exact nature of creativity is still unknown (just as the exact nature of intelligence is unknown, for that matter). Secondly, creativity is best thought of as a complex process which involves a cluster of techniques and a characteristic approach to problems, rather than as a thing or a quantity. Teaching for creativity, then, involves emphasis on the finding of solutions to new problems through a reappraisal of the known, the extending of thinking into 'illogical' and divergent areas, the deducing of previously unseen relationships between apparently separate domains of experience, and so on, rather than the transmission of a known corpus of knowledge about creativity, or the teaching of a definable creative skill. Consequently, the question with which this section is concerned is really that of whether appropriate teaching methods can foster (1) the transfer of training across subjects; (2) the finding of unifying principles which demonstrate the relatedness of segments of knowledge usually held to be separate; (3) the ability to see the 'facts' in a new light and to question what is usually held to be self-evidently true; and (4) the ability to see analogies and to exercise imagination, since these are the kinds of skills which contribute to the process of creative thinking.

SOME USEFUL RESEARCH

A number of studies have investigated the relationship between teaching methods and the fostering of creative skills, and the results are encouraging. Maltzman, Bogartz and Breger (1958), for example, demonstrated an increase in the originality of responses to the 'Unusual Uses' test with appropriate training, and Maltzman also demonstrated in a second study (Maltzman, Simon, Raskin and Licht, 1960) that this effect persisted over time and did not just apply to immediate readministration of the test. Parnes and Meadow (1959) showed that training in 'brainstorming' increased scores on creative problem-solving, and also (Parnes and Meadow, 1960) that the improvement persisted even as much as four years after the training had been given. Another useful finding on this point was made by Suchman who taught two groups of science students in the fifth and sixth grades for a twenty-four week period. The first group (the experimental group) was taught by the method of 'inquiry training' which means that they were taught by being given problems (in physics) to solve for themselves. The role of the teacher was merely to answer 'Yes' or 'No' to the students' queries and not to give them ready-made answers. The second group (the control group) was taught by conventional methods, which involved provision of facts by the teacher and learning of these by the students. At the end of twenty-four weeks there were no differences between groups in understanding of physics, but the experimental group was markedly more inclined to be curious and inquiring. In fact, Suchman concluded that the training had a strong effect on question-asking fluency of the experimental group. They were more highly motivated to learn than were the controls, and they seemed to enjoy the learning process, two highly desirable end results in the eyes of most teachers, which support the notion that creative learning is intrinsically motivated.

TWO ESPECIALLY IMPORTANT STUDIES

A definitive study with primary school children has been reported by Torrance (1961). He set out to show whether children in the first three grades could be taught to produce ideas by the use of appropriate teaching methods, and he found that in the second and third grades, trained children consistently surpassed untrained on all the measures of creativity which he employed. He concluded that schoolchildren '. . . can in a short time be taught a set of principles that will enable them to produce more and better ideas than they would have without training'.[1]

There was a further important aspect of Torrance's findings, however, which should be emphasised at this juncture. He also compared the effect of instructing the children merely to produce large numbers of responses, without regard to quality, with the effect of instructing them to produce clever, interesting and unusual ideas. Surprisingly enough, instructions which asked for mere massive quantities of answers without

[1] Torrance, E. P., 'Priming creative thinking in the primary grades', *Elementary School Journal,* 1961.

any concern for their quality elicited fewer responses than instructions to be clever and unusual. This indicates that it was the quality of the ideas which really aroused the interest of the children, since they were more easily taught to make clever, novel and effective answers (i.e., creative productions) than merely to churn out large amounts of everyday material. Hence the effect of the training was both to increase the quantity of response making, and more important, to improve its quality. This finding is also consistent with the assertion made earlier in this chapter, that creative learning is better motivated than conventional learning, since the children worked more effectively when producing creative responses.

POSSIBILITY OF INDIRECT TEACHING OF CREATIVITY

Finally, Torrance (1965a, pp.80-3) has demonstrated that creative thinking scores increase sharply, even without specific training, when the teacher is himself interested in and aware of creativity. The children involved in this study included all members of twenty classes in a single elementary school. They were tested for creative thinking ability in January and again in May, after being divided into two groups consisting on the one hand of those children whose teachers scored high on an index of 'creativity motivation' (i.e., whose teachers were anxious to foster creativity), and on the other of those whose teachers were mainly 'power motivated' (i.e., who sought firm discipline and clear understanding of 'the rules', who were critical of 'stupid' questions, and so on). At three grade levels, the first involving children at kindergarten level, the second grades one to three, and the third grades four to six, the relative number of children taught by the creativity-motivated teachers who had increased their scores at the retest was compared with the proportion of those taught by the power-motivated who had improved. At both the kindergarten level and the grades one to three level, the students taught by the creativity-motivated teachers included significantly more children who had gained on the creative thinking test than those taught by the power-motivated teachers. There was no significant difference at the grade four to six level.

It is also interesting to look at the children who actually made substantial decreases in their creative thinking scores, and to consider these separately from the children who either gained or made only small losses. Again and again, Torrance points out, these children came from the group whose teachers' critical and control motivation exceeded their creativity motivation. Thus this study provides evidence that creativity can be taught not only by directly seeking to increase its incidence, as studies cited earlier suggest, but even merely by the contact of children with teachers who are conscious of creativity and eager to foster it in their students. Conversely, creative thinking can be inhibited readily by teachers whose main interest is in authority, logic and control.

AN ANSWER

The question of whether creativity can actually be taught has been conceived, in this section, as really asking whether the classroom teacher can increase certain 'divergent' knowledge-getting strategies in his students. These strategies involve the student in relying not on the finding of set answers readymade in the world of all-knowing teachers and infallible textbooks, but on the finding of solutions through the use of his own powers of inquiry, curiosity and independence, and through his ability to draw together domains of his experience which have not previously been seen to be related. When the solutions he reaches through these means are relevant, and correct in the sense that they have parsimony and grace, they reflect high levels of true creativity. The answer to this question may be stated in a generalisation which summarises the contents of the present section: The capacity of students to think creatively and to learn creatively can be fostered by the classroom teacher. He can achieve this by applying appropriate teaching techniques or even by merely being alert to the existence of creative learning as distinct from rote- and authority-centred learning.

How can Creative Learning be Fostered?

THE QUESTION

It is all very well to point out that utilisation of the divergent powers of children leads to intrinsically motivated learning and, furthermore, that appropriate teaching can either inhibit or facilitate the tendency of students to learn creatively. However, at this juncture it is apparent that an examination of the techniques by which creative learning can be fostered is needed. The teacher may well ask how this is to be achieved, and the question is a good one. First, however, it is necessary to examine the way in which many teachers block the development and use of creativity in their students' learning.

ANTI-CREATIVE ASPECTS OF THE CONVENTIONAL CLASSROOM

The conventional classroom is oriented towards successful solution of clearly defined problems through finding the 'right' answer. The teacher is assumed to be in a position to provide an authoritative, 'correct' solution if he chooses to do so, and it is implicit in the interaction between teacher, pupil and subject matter that logic, facts, and laws will provide answers to all problems. In fact, the usual task with which the student finds himself faced is of 'zeroing-in' on a uniquely determined, lawful 'answer' to a fully defined, clearly presented problem. The role of the teacher in such a classroom is to provide the student with the correct technique on the first occasion that a new problem is encountered, and then to see to it that the child reproduces the recently demonstrated technique when next he comes across a similar problem.

In such teaching, when it is carried to its extreme limits, the emphasis is upon learning of discrete facts more or less for their own sake, excessive concern with the importance of memorisation, repeated drill of material which must be memorised, mechanical learning of set, invariable and presumably task-unique techniques of problem solving, and an uneconomical and stultifying preoccupation with rote-learning as a means of acquiring knowledge.

An important distinction which is overlooked in this kind of classroom is the difference between the presented problem and the discovered problem; the difference between the presented solution and the discovered solution; the difference between the produced product and the merely reproduced product. Such a classroom is based on the supposition that no knowledge other than that which is embodied in accepted facts and laws is valid, and that it is impossible for the student to benefit from what he does not know in the same way as he benefits from what he is able to regurgitate at will. Learning acquired in classrooms tending towards this kind of teaching will seem to be discrete and unrelated to other areas of knowledge: it is the common and salutary experience of many teachers to be told, for example, when they suggest that an angle of unknown size in a geometry problem be labelled 'x': 'You can't do that, Sir. X is algebra.'

WHAT THE CLASSROOM SHOULD PROVIDE

In fact, far from being like the one stereotyped in the preceding paragraphs, classroom procedures ought to lay great emphasis on the importance of *discovering* both problems and solutions. It should emphasise that skills acquired in the one situation may be transformed until they are suitable for use in different situations. It should emphasise that there are often many ways of reaching a solution to one given problem, so that the child is capable of responding to one situation in a variety of ways. The present author has been present in classrooms where a child has offered an alternative approach, which differs from that given in the textbook, to some problem. Too often the teacher's response has been to deride the child's suggestion, and even to end by insisting that the orthodox technique be adhered to 'Because I say so', or 'Because that's the way they do it in the textbook, and if you think you are smarter than the book you'd better think again'.

To generalise, then, the classroom should encourage the

child to recognise the existence of and seek alternative solutions to problems, and should play down the importance of the teacher and the text as omniscient providers of fixed and inflexible 'correct' solutions. The teacher should be willing to introduce new and unknown elements into the curriculum and to entertain ideas which may even be unknown either to himself or the textbook. His aim should be to give the student the feel of creating knowledge, so that he is imaginative and cognitively flexible.

Some Specific Practices Antagonistic to Creativity

EMPHASIS ON BEING RIGHT

The most prized achievement to which any pupil can aspire in the conventional classroom is success, and success usually means hitting upon what the sources of 'correct' solutions (teacher and textbook) regard as right. It is generally a better thing for a student to give a safe answer which he knows will be successful than to risk a rebuff and failure by trying an experimental answer. Worse, the teacher may even be annoyed by questions and may rebuff the exploring child, or he may wholely or partly ignore issues raised in the interests of time and the needs of the rest of the class. In fact, the emphasis is on scrupulous accuracy, and agreeing with external authorities.

EXTERNAL EVALUATION

The habit of seeking always to be right in terms of external criteria is encouraged by the fact that schoolchildren more or less permanently find themselves under conditions where what they produce is being evaluated by someone other than themselves and in terms of criteria other than the satisfaction-giving qualities of the product. Evaluation tends to be completely externalised, rigidly power oriented and strictly logical. In such a situation, the child is trained to seek close resemblance between his own school work and the ideal format provided by the teacher and the textbook.

TEACHERS' IMPATIENCE WITH TIMEWASTING

A question whose point is not immediately apparent, or an answer whose logic is obscure is likely to be seen by the teacher as either a piece of foolishness or an attempt to waste time (as indeed, they sometimes are). He is pressed by the requirement of getting through a set amount of work in a given lesson and there usually is not time to follow up the peculiarities of any one child, who may well be regarded as a nuisance in any case (see Chapter 5). Furthermore, the teacher is himself working in a highly convergent system, and finds himself subject to external evaluation and so on, so that he is under pressure to get on with the job. Thus, divergent behaviour which results in loss of time is frequently frowned upon.

CONFORMITY PRESSURES

Especially by secondary school level, children are under increasing pressure to conform to the behaviours of their peer-group. The pressure of their classmates is towards uniformity of behaviour and it is a grave thing to find oneself marked off as different, even when the difference lies in upsetting the closed system of logic-orientation which prevails in most classroooms. This pressure to conform is reinforced by the school authorities and by individual teachers who require uniform format for written work, standardised approaches to specific situations, and so on. The situation is so extreme in some schools that it is an enormous offence for a child to be anything other than a colourless copy of his fellow students—any divergence in classroom behaviour is seen as a sign of abnormality and is likely to make the child feel like an outsider.

SHARP DISTINCTION BETWEEN WORK AND PLAY

A very clever distinction is drawn between work and play in both our culture and our schools. Work is stern and demanding, play is frivolous and light and the two never overlap. Thus, the child is given to understand that free use of imagination, testing of the limits of logic and sense, humour and lightheartedness do not belong in the serious setting of the classroom. The present author has seen a grammar school boy of thirteen or fourteen caned for smiling in assembly; the headmaster was horrified to think that a child might, somehow, see something to smile to himself about in the serious business of an assembly of the entire school. The boy was lectured in front of the whole student body along the lines of 'I'll teach you that school isn't a laughing matter, or even a smiling matter, my lad', and then flogged as a warning to the rest of the students that they must get out of their heads any nonsense about smiling during serious matters. The result of this clear distinction between work and play is that activity which is seen as work is seldom informed by the spirit of adventurousness and inquiry which is characteristic of play activity, so that work becomes formalised and stilted.

How can the Teacher Overcome these Factors?

A GENERALISATION

Basically, the teacher's task is to encourage willingness to look outside the safe world of authority in his students. Ideally, they would be skilled and willing at perceiving non-explicit problems in their school work, and they should be able to bring the same free play of ideas which informs play activity to the serious business of the classrooom. In the case of being right, for example, it should be made apparent to students that there are frequently more ways than one of being right and that, as a matter of fact, being right is not always as important as getting a feel for the organisation and style of knowledge. Courageous mistakes often promote better understanding of basic principles than pedestrian correctness, and learning is frequently fostered as effectively by an incorrect answer as by a correct one. This is especially true when the incorrect answer represents a beginning attempt at applying some general principles which have been partly discerned, rather than a blind parrotting of an answer which is known to be correct, although the reason why is obscure. It is, in fact, sometimes better to be wrong but know why than to be right but not know why.

However, any suggestion that evaluation of students' production should be a matter of self-evaluation rather than external evaluation immediately comes up against the question of whether self-evaluation means letting the students do exactly as they like. There is no intention in this section of proposing that the teacher should so completely abdicate his position as evaluator of end products that classroom control is reduced to a matter of children doing as they please. On the contrary, it is reasonable to suppose that an adult teacher with years more experience and training than the schoolchild is very much more likely to be able to make worthwhile judgments of the value of students' work. If he is not, then it is doubtful whether he is entitled to keep the job he holds. Thus, there is the question of how the teacher is to maintain his role as leader and to give the students the benefit of his superior training and experience, without at the same time making them authority-oriented and convergent. In fact, while strictly logical evaluation on the basis of criteria external to the student is an inhibitor of creative learning, a *laissez faire* situation is equally bad.

GUIDED SELF-EVALUATION

Torrance (1965a, p.174) has drawn attention to a technique which avoids the pitfalls inherent in the teacher abdicating his position as leader of the class, and at the same time enables him to foster the creative thinking abilities of his pupils. The approach which he has recommended may appropriately be referred to as 'guided self-evaluation'. Guided self-evaluation involves two main principles, *acceptance* and *approval.* Basically, acceptance consists in being willing to entertain students' ideas, even when they are apparently contrary to established principles. It should seem to the student that his ideas are being regarded as having a legitimate existence, regardless of their rightness or wrongness in terms of external logical criteria. In other words, the emphasis should be on the production of ideas rather than merely of correct solutions, so that an idea may have an existence for its own sake and not merely as a specific attempt to resolve a single given problem.

Approval involves an extension of the notion of acceptance, in that the child should be given to understand that the teacher is glad to have his idea and welcomes it with pleasure. This position is the opposite of that seen in many classrooms where the child's tentative idea-producing efforts are met with anything from amused contempt to impatient sneering, since they interrupt the flow of wisdom from the lectern and waste time which could be spent in rote-learning correct ways of doing things.

Again, at this stage it may begin to seem as though what is being advocated is that students be encouraged to do as they like. On the contrary, there is a place for criticism of ineffective, non-relevant productions, even within the system advocated here. The point is that criticism should always be associated with strong expressions of approval, so that the criticism is not seen as a rejection of the proposal put forward. In indicating faults the teacher should aim at getting the child to deduce his own shortcomings rather than bringing them directly to the child's attention. For example, this can be done by adopting the following approach: 'Yes that's good. Can you think of any ways to improve what you have suggested? I think I can, but I'd like to hear what you think about it.' And so on.

When this approach fails to bring shortcomings to light because the child is unable to see any way in which the solution offered can be improved, the teacher may take a further step and adopt an approach which is what Torrance (1965a, p.216) calls 'trouble-shooting', rather than authoritative and answer-giving. Thus, he may draw the child's attention to deficiencies in an indirect way, as for example in the following: 'The experiment you have suggested is promising, but would that part there really work? What do you think?'[1] This approach is to be contrasted with that of the teacher who starts a lesson by observing something like: 'Today I'm going to tell you all about ...', or 'Open your books at page 12. This shows how you can ...', and so on. The same kind of teacher might greet an erroneous solution suggested by a child with remarks like: 'No that's wrong. How many times have I told you that it's impossible to ...' 'If you'd looked at page 94 you'd have known that you can't do that. It says there ...'

SUMMARY: SUGGESTIONS AT THE PRACTICAL LEVEL

To sum up, basically what is required is a classroom in which the notion of one and only one 'right' way of doing things has been destroyed. In such a classroom, it should be a prized and legitimate activity to produce ideas and invent responses rather than merely to reproduce what the teacher has fed in. The child should be given to understand that it is acceptable both to the teacher and the whole class group to seek solutions for oneself, to question and inquire, to wonder and suppose.

At this point it is appropriate to conclude the present section by putting forward some suggestions of what the teacher should try to do in his classroom in order to encourage and foster creative learning. Torrance (1962b)[2] has suggested twenty ways in which the teacher can nurture creativity. Some of them are:

1 Value creative thinking.
2 Encourage manipulation of objects and ideas.
3 Develop tolerance of new ideas.
4 Beware of forcing a set pattern.

[1] The procedures involved in so-called 'trouble-shooting' evaluation thus resemble closely the activities being measured in the Product Improvement Test (see p.106). In this test, which is one part of the Minnesota battery of tests of creative thinking, the child is given some object (for example, a toy dog) and asked of ways in which it could be improved so that it would be more fun, more interesting, etc.

[2] Torrance, E. P., 'Developing creative thinking through school experiences', in Parnes, S. J. and Harding, H. F., *A sourcebook for creative thinking*. Scribners.

5 Teach the child to value his creative thinking.
6 Encourage and evaluate self-initiated learning.
7 Make available resources for working out ideas.
8 Develop skills of constructive criticism.
9 Encourage acquisition of knowledge in a variety of fields.
10 Be adventurous-spirited yourself.

The final suggestion may well be taken as a general exhortation to all teachers and parents.

The Creative Teacher

A DESCRIPTION

In the previous section, some precepts for creativity-oriented teachers to follow were suggested. One might well ask what kind of teachers result when they do, in fact, actively foster their own creativity. Several studies of highly creative teachers cast some light on this query. Among such studies, Torrance (1962a, pp.193-6) has discussed three in considerable detail (Hobelman, 1957; Barkan, 1960; Wessel, 1961), and he has proposed some generalisations emphasising the characteristics common to all of the many different creative teachers described by those three authors. From these generalisations, it is possible to extract a description of the creative teacher, and it seems appropriate to end this book with such a description.

In their classroom behaviours, creative teachers are 'resourceful, flexible, and willing to "get off the beaten track" '. In particular, they display a very high level of ability to form good relationships with highly creative students in their classes, although they usually enjoy good relations with other children as well. This last point is rather surprising when one examines their personalities.

They tend, in out-of-school life, and in their relationships with their colleagues, to be nonconforming and even discontented and fault-finding. They frequently take on tasks that are too much for them, as a result of their willingness to tackle really difficult problems and, consequently, they experience a good deal of failure. This may lead to disappointment and irritability as, of course, they cannot be right all the time. Consequently, they may seem short-tempered and even boorish to their fellow teachers. Thus, the highly creative teacher is a bit like the highly creative student. He is sometimes a nuisance or even an embarrassment to his colleagues and often causes them discomfort. Nevertheless, as with the highly creative student, we ought to be capable of recognising and appreciating his qualities, and of encouraging him if, in fact, we cannot be like him.

APPENDIX A

A Canadian Study

At various places in the text, reference has been made to a study conducted in Canada by the present author. Although details of the study and of the findings have been reported elsewhere (Cropley, 1965; Cropley, 1966; Anderson and Cropley, 1966; Cropley, 1967), a brief description of the children involved and of how the findings mentioned in the text were obtained is relevant, at this point.

The subjects involved were 320 grade seven children from a prairie city in Canada, who took the battery of tests described here in June 1964. Their mean age was thirteen years six months, and mean Lorge–Thorndike verbal IQ 114·3 (SD = 14·5). The mean verbal IQ for 170 boys was 114·7 (SD = 15·2) and the corresponding figure for the 150 girls was 113·8 (SD = 13·6).

The tests administered fell into three groups—tests of creativity, conventional tests of convergent thinking, and non-intellective tests.

TESTS OF CREATIVITY

Six Guilford–Torrance tests were administered. The verbal ones included Seeing Problems (Guilford), Tin Can Uses (Guilford, modified by Torrance), and Consequences (Guilford), while the non-verbal ones were Symbol Production (Guilford), Concealed Figures (devised by ETS and accepted by Guilford), and Circles (Torrance). A local version of Mednick's Remote Associations Test was also administered, although the fact that each item has, almost always, only one correct answer appears to make it a convergent test. This possibility is reinforced by the consideration that each item represents an intersect problem, the answer to which is nearly always completely determined by the constraints of previous information.

TESTS OF CONVENTIONAL CONVERGENT THINKING

Scores were obtained on six measures of convergent thinking. These included (1) verbal and non-verbal IQs from the appropriate forms of the Lorge–Thorndike tests; (2) the academic average of each child for core courses; and (3) three measures from French's (1963) kit of reference tests for cognitive factors, Vocabulary, Inferences, and Shortest Road.

NON-INTELLECTIVE MEASURES

A number of non-intellective tests were administered, including tests of conformity, category width, impulse expression and risk taking. The impulse expression test consisted of items which expressed a strong impulse at odds with more acceptable positions. It was assumed, following Luria's (1963) theorising about the role of speech in regulating behaviour, that the extent to which the subjects chose to act out their impulses would be inversely related to the extent to which they controlled their own impulses through the use of internal (adult) verbal rules. A sample item is given here. 'A friend asks you over to hear some new records after school, and you want to go. Which would you be most likely to say to yourself?

1 I must make sure that I'm not late home.
2 I must do my homework before I go.
3 My mother is expecting me to come straight home from school.
4 I'll go along and have a good time. I can worry later.'

Finally a test of socio-economic status was also administered (MacArthur and Elley, 1963).

PROCEDURE

The scoring of protocols was carried out according to the published specifications, wherever this was possible, except in the case of four tests of 'creativity' which were scored for originality only.[1] This scoring method involved allotting weights (Torrance, 1963, p.72) to the responses to each item of each test, the highest weights going to the least common responses. Accordingly, Consequences, Seeing Problems, Uses, and Circles were scored in this way using the following weights: responses appearing on more than 15 per cent of protocols—0; responses appearing between 7 and 15 per cent—1; responses appearing from 3 to 6 per cent—2; responses appearing either 1 or 2 per cent of the time—3; responses appearing less than 1 per cent—4. In all cases, it was necessary for a response to be task appropriate for it to score any points at all. This procedure weights adaptive, statistically uncommon responses and scores are thus argued to reflect originality with a high level of validity.

A Principal Axis factor analysis was carried out on the matrix of intercorrelations among the thirteen intellective variables (the seven divergent thinking tests plus the six conventional, convergent thinking tests). A plot of the unrotated loadings of the first two factors revealed that the clusters of convergent and divergent variables were not independent of one another, and the axes were rotated into an oblique relationship. On the basis of the loadings for the creativity factor, factor scores were computed for each student, and the correlates of performance on this variable were studied. This was done by selecting two groups of subjects on the basis of their factor scores, the first group (the high creatives) consisting of the 10 per cent of the whole sample highest on creativity, the second (the low creatives) of the 10 per cent lowest on creativity. The relevant results have been referred to in appropriate places in the text.

[1] See Appendix B, p.101.

APPENDIX B

Creativity Tests

The basic position adopted in this book, so far as intellectual testing is concerned, may be summarised as follows: intellect is a pervasive and generalised phenomenon whose presence can only be inferred from the observation of behaviour. It has been customary, in the past, to sample it by the use of IQ tests and to quantify it on the form of an IQ. As a result of this, many psychologists have come to behave as though human intellect is restricted to the kinds of skills sampled by conventional IQ tests. However, this point of view has recently been challenged. In particular, Guilford (1950) has drawn attention to the fact that people may think not only in a convergent way which 'zeroes-in' on a single correct answer to some lawful and circumscribed problem, but also in a divergent way which results in the production of many and varied answers. The former kind of thinking is referred to as 'convergent thinking', the latter as 'divergent thinking'.

Examination of the kinds of items included in the usual IQ tests indicates that they concentrate heavily on items which require thinking of the convergent kind, and neglect the divergent kind. Thus, it has become necessary for psychologists who are interested in divergent thinking to construct new tests aimed at eliciting a divergent kind of thinking. Virtually all the research cited in this book, whether the authors reported the results as concerning divergent thinking or creativity, employed tests of this latter kind in order to identify highly creative children, and consequently some information concerning what creativity tests are like is useful to the reader. For this reason, three major groups of creativity tests will be discussed in some detail.

1 Guilford-type Tests of Creativity

Attempts to measure the kinds of skills important in divergent thinking have been going on for some time. As early as 1922 Simpson (1922) pointed out that the IQ test neglected some aspects of human intellectual functioning, and attempted to construct some tests of creativity. Andrews (1930) designed tests of 'imagination', McCloy and Meier (1931) utilised a test of 'recreative imagination', and Welch (1946) tested the ability of university students to make original combinations of ideas. Nevertheless, it was the work of Guilford (1950; 1959) which really established the study of divergent thinking and creativity, and the Guilford approach to its measurement will be outlined in some detail.

Guilford (1959) argued that there are three main dimensions of intellect, which he labelled 'operations', 'products', and 'contents'. In other words, he suggested that three basic dimensions are needed fully to describe an intellectual task. One needs to know (1) what kind of material is being processed (contents); (2) what is being done to it (operations); and (3) what kind of result this leads to (products). Hence any intellectual task will elicit particular kinds of *operations* which are carried out on the *contents* of the task and lead to a certain kind of *products.* He has identified five kinds of operations (cognition, memory, divergent productions, convergent productions, and evaluation), which are carried out on four possible kinds of contents (figural, semantic, symbolic, behavioural), and may lead to one of six kinds of product (units, classes, relations, systems, transformations, implications). Thus, a test which requires the subject to notice that wheat, barley, and oats are all cereals, would involve semantic contents (words), which would have to be subjected to convergent productions ('zeroing-in' on the common elements), to lead to a class (category, i.e. 'cereals') as a product. Altogether, there would thus be 120 possible factors of intellect (4×5×6).

FACTORS OF INTELLECT IMPORTANT FOR CREATIVITY

The factors of intellect which Guilford regards as important in creativity include sensitivity to problems, word fluency, ideational fluency, semantic flexibility, associational fluency and originality, among others. For each factor which he regarded as important in creativity Guilford has designed one or more appropriate tests. Thus, to test for sensitivity to problems, for example, he has suggested the *Seeing Problems* test which requires subjects to list problems which might arise in connection with some common object, like say a tree. Word fluency is measured in tests like *Suffixes,* or *Prefixes,* ideational fluency is measured by tests like *Thing Categories,* semantic flexibility by *Uses,* associational fluency by *Controlled Associations,* and originality by *Consequences* or *Symbol Production,* and so on. A number of these tests will be discussed in detail in the following sections of this chapter.

SEEING PROBLEMS

Items in this test include common objects like 'a tree'. Instructions to the subject ask him to write down as many interesting and unusual problems as he can think of which might arise in connection with the item. Thus, acceptable responses to 'a tree' might include answers like 'What will you do with it, now that you've got it?' (a common answer) or 'How would you go about getting a licence to rent parts of it to nesting birds?' (an uncommon answer) and so on.

SUFFIXES AND PREFIXES

These two tests require the subjects to write as many words as they can think of which begin with a given prefix, like say ITS (*Prefixes*), or to write as many words as they can think of which end with a specified suffix like say ELT (*Suffixes*). In this case, as the emphasis is on fluency (i.e., sheer number of responses), there is no strict need for an injunction to make responses as unusual as possible although, clearly, the child who can think of unusual words will probably give the highest number of responses.

THING CATEGORIES

Subjects are required to list the names of as many things as they can which are, say, 'round'. Again, the test is designed to measure chiefly fluency and so the instructions emphasise sheer number of responses rather than quality, although unusual responses will, naturally, tend to increase the total number of responses produced.

USES

In the original version of this test, subjects were required to write down as many interesting and unusual uses they could think of for common items like a hammer or a brick. Torrance (1962a, p.46) has extended this test by suggesting that a tin can is particularly appropriate for use with young children. The kind of response most frequently met for a tin includes answers like 'water container', 'saucepan', 'to throw', 'plant-pot', or 'rattle'. Less common responses include 'food for a hungry goat', 'portable toilet', or 'outer shell for a mouse's rocketship' and so on.[1]

CONTROLLED ASSOCIATIONS

Subjects are given a word and required to write down as many synonyms for it as they can think of. A further version of this test involves giving two words and asking the child to write

[1] Of course, the commonness of responses is a function of the subject's culture. Thus, in Australia, a common response suggesting a possible use for a tin can is 'a wicket for a game of cricket'. In Canada, on the other hand, this response was made by only one student, and he was an immigrant at that. Hence what may be a common response in one group of subjects may be extremely uncommon in another.

down a third word which links the two. For example, suppose that the two words are 'emerald' and 'young'. The third word might be 'green'. This latter version is called *Associations IV* in the Guilford test battery.

CONSEQUENCES

The test describes several unusual situations which might conceivably arise in the world, and invites the child to write down as many interesting and unusual possible consequences of the event as he can think of. For example, items include 'What would happen if it started raining and never stopped?' Common responses include 'We'd all get very wet', 'The price of umbrellas would go up', or 'We'd have to live on hilltops.' Uncommon responses include answers like 'Tibet would get awfully crowded', or 'Diving suits would go up in price.' One poignant note was touched upon by a student in response to the item: 'What would happen if people lost their feelings for each other?' He wrote: 'No more love. No more marriage. No more children. *No more me.*'

SYMBOL PRODUCTION

In this test, the subject is presented with a page divided into twelve boxes, by appropriately placed vertical and horizontal lines. Each box contains a short statement like 'A man walking', or 'An aeroplane taking off', and at later stages, items like 'Anger', or 'Pride'. The subject is required to insert a brief pencil drawing which suggests the content of the statement in a symbolic way. A mere literal representation will not receive any credit, so that a drawing of a walking man is not acceptable for 'A man walking'.

2 *The Minnesota Tests of Creative Thinking*

SOME MINNESOTA TESTS

On the basis of modifications and extensions to the Guilford-type tests, a large number of creativity tests has been devised at the University of Minnesota, some of them quite different from the kind of tests Guilford first designed. Among the Minnesota tests are the *Ask and Guess Test,* the *Product Improvement Test,* and *Creative Writing Tests* and the *Just Suppose Test.* The Minnesota battery (The Minnesota Tests of Creative Thinking) also includes a number of tests of a non-verbal nature, including the *Incomplete Figures Test,* the *Circles Test,* the *Squares Test,* and the *Shapes Test.* Torrance (1962a) has reported that among the advantages of the Minnesota tests is the fact that they have been found suitable for use with subjects ranging from kindergarten to post-graduate studies. These tests are briefly described in the following sections of this chapter.

ASK AND GUESS TEST

This test first requires the subject to ask questions about a picture which he is shown, questions which cannot be answered merely by looking at the picture, which is usually a Mother Goose print. He may also be asked to make guesses about events preceding and immediately following the scene depicted. Scoring may be carried out for fluency, flexibility and originality.

PRODUCT IMPROVEMENT TEST

In this test subjects are shown a common toy, usually either a stuffed dog or a stuffed monkey, and they are asked to think of changes which would make the toy more fun. They are then asked to invent as many unusual uses of the toy as they can think of. Scoring may be for flexibility, for inventive level or for originality.

CREATIVE WRITING TESTS

Subjects are given a list of ten or so topics and asked to write a story about one of them. The topics involve people or animals with unusual qualities like a flying monkey, or a crying man.

JUST SUPPOSE TEST

This test resembles Guilford's *Consequences* test in that the subject is asked to predict the probable outcomes of an unusual situation. However, in the case of the Minnesota test, the situation is not merely described verbally, but the child is also presented with a drawing of the situation. Items include situations like 'Just suppose I went through the wringer and came out flat.' Responses are scored for fluency, flexibility and originality.

INCOMPLETE FIGURES TEST

Subjects are required to finish off incompleted drawings, which are presented to them as the test material. The test is thought to measure three dimensions—penetration, elaboration and originality.

CIRCLES AND SQUARES

In these tests subjects are presented with a page on which, in one form, thirty-five circles have been drawn. The circles are not elaborated on in any way, so that the subject is confronted with a page full of rings. The instructions require him to draw as many interesting and unusual things as he can think of in which the circle forms an integral part. Underneath he is asked to write the name of the object. Common responses include a plate, a monocle, a button, a balloon, a wheel, and so on. Uncommon responses include a human nose, seen from directly underneath where say a fly sitting on your upper lip would be, a man in the stocks, and so on. The other form involves the same format except that squares are substituted for circles. Scoring is for fluency, flexibility and originality.

SHAPES TEST (PICTURE CONSTRUCTION TEST)

This test requires subjects to create a picture, using standardised shapes of coloured paper as the base stimulus, and making the paper shapes an integral part of the picture. The instructions require the subject to make up as highly elaborated and unusual a picture as they can. They are also asked to make up titles for their pictures, as they are in the Incomplete Figures Test. Scoring of this test is, again, along a number of dimensions including elaboration, communication and originality, among others. It was the Shapes Test which was administered to Kathy, and which formed the basis of her selection for special study.

All of the Minnesota tasks are described in much greater detail by Torrance (1962a, pp.213-53), and anyone who wishes to make use of them would be well advised to consult the text. In general, there are alternative forms of each test available, so that two complete Minnesota batteries (Form A and Form B) exist.

3 *Scoring of Creativity Tests*

As Torrance (1963, p.72) has pointed out, in general both Guilford-type and Minnesota-type creativity tests may be scored for fluency, flexibility, or originality, and indeed for some other dimensions too. Fluency, as used here, means merely that the total number of responses may be recorded, while flexibility refers to the number of switches of category which are made. For example, 'saucepan' and 'drinking cup' are two different responses to the *Tin Can Uses Test,* and would count as two answers for the purposes of scoring for fluency. On the other hand, both are concerned with the fact that a tin can is capable of holding a liquid, and hence constitute only a single response for the purposes of flexibility scoring.

However, there are serious difficulties involved in scoring creativity tests. The term 'creativity' has, as has already been pointed out, cultural overtones and just what is creative is partly determined by the particular society (Dentler and Mackler, 1962). Furthermore, the claim that a response is creative usually involves aesthetic or professional criteria (Maltzmann, 1960), while in any case the long-term ability of criteria like fluency and flexibility to predict creative performance in later life is unknown. A project analogous to Terman's (1925) intelligence study, in which he selected a group of highly intelligent subjects and followed them up over a period of nearly forty years, would be needed to establish that creativity tests can predict performance in later life.

Furthermore, both Mackler (1962) and Wodtke (1964) have shown that creativity tests have unsatisfactorily low reliabilities.[1] Hence the scoring of creativity tests is complicated by two problems—the tests are of doubtful validity (i.e., no one is certain that they really measure creativity, because ideas of what is creative differ so much from person to person and from culture to culture), and they are unreliable. Hence what is needed is a scoring method for creativity tests which provides an objective way of judging the extent to which responses are novel; the notion of originality is proposed as an approach which satisfies this requirement.

SCORING FOR ORIGINALITY

Scoring for originality involves allotting weights to subjects' test responses according to the frequency with which the responses are present in the answers of some criterion group. Thus, if a ten-year-old child gives an answer to the *Tin Can Uses Test* which is extremely unusual in a sample of, say 200 ten-year-olds, he receives a high score for the answer. On the other hand, common answers get little or no credit. Modifying the weights suggested by Torrance (1963, p.72), the present author has employed the following set of weights in his own work; responses given by more than 15 per cent of the responding group—0; responses given by 7 to 15 per cent of the group—1 point; responses given by 3 to 6 per cent inclusive—2 points; responses given by 1 or 2 per cent of the group—3

[1] The reliability of a test is a measure of the extent to which the same person tends to get the same score as before, if he takes the test a second time.

points; responses given by less than 1 per cent of the group—4 points.[1]

This procedure involves, in effect, giving high scores to those children whose answers are the most unusual by comparison with some peer-group (all members of the same class, for example, or all children in one school, and so on). It necessitates double marking of all tests, first to compute the frequency with which each answer appears and then after weights have been allotted to each answer, to score each child's answer to each question. The method is time-consuming but, unfortunately, when one is dealing with an essentially non-mechanical process like creative thinking, mechanical methods of scoring are of little use.

4 *Some Recent Criticisms of Creativity Tests*

It has already been pointed out that creativity tests are of unknown ability to make long-range predictions, while there is some doubt as to their reliability too. A third related criticism has resulted from attempts to show that tests of the Guilford–Torrance type measure something which is not measured by IQ tests, for these attempts have met with very limited success. Although a great deal has been written on this topic, the best summary of criticisms, on the grounds that existing creativity tests are not much more than a slightly different kind of IQ test, is to be found in a recent book by Wallach and Kogan (1965). They have pointed out that again and again relationships among creativity tests, which are supposed to be measuring something common to them but distinct from IQ tests, are

[1] Some readers may be puzzled by the fact that the widths of these score intervals, expressed as percentages, are apparently uneven, i.e., the one point category courses a spread of 7 per cent to 15 per cent. Why does not the next category also involve the same spread? In fact, the point-score categories are based on the normal distribution, and the percentage limits for each category correspond to equal standard-score distances along the *x*-axis of a normal curve. Thus, the distance between 7 per cent and 13 per cent is about 0·44 standard deviations, as is the distance from 3 per cent to 6 per cent and so on.

weaker than relationships between creativity tests and IQ tests. This is even true in some of the definitive studies in the area, like those of Getzels and Jackson or of Torrance.

Consequently, there is considerable doubt that the kinds of tests described in earlier sections satisfy the requirements of what is needed in tests of creativity, if the study of the area is to proceed with any confidence. Nevertheless, Wallach and Kogan do not conclude that nothing can be done in the matter of testing creativity. They have, in fact, designed a battery of tests, heavily dependent on the existing tests derived from the work of Guilford, Torrance, and associates, but avoiding some of the weaknesses which have reduced the effectiveness of older tests. Although these creativity tests have been described in full detail elsewhere (Wallach and Kogan, 1965, pp.28-50), they will be briefly reviewed here.

WALLACH AND KOGAN'S TESTS OF CREATIVITY

These authors report three verbal tests, which they called *Instances, Alternate Uses,* and *Similarities,* while they also employed two tests in which the test material was visual rather than verbal. The two visual tests were called *Pattern Meanings* and *Line Meanings.* Common to all five of these tests were several important administrational procedures which were argued by their authors to be of critical importance in their effectiveness. All the tests were administered individually with no time limit, none of them required the children to write down anything (recording of responses was done by the tester), and, most important of all, the tests were presented to the children as games, and a real effort was made to maintain the playful atmosphere throughout testing.

In the case of *Instances,* the child was required to generate possible instances of a class of objects specified by the tester. For example, he might be asked to name as many round things as he could think of. *Alternative Uses* involved the child who was being tested in inventing as many uses as he could think of for common objects like a newspaper or a knife, while in *Similarities* he was required to name as many ways as he could think of in which specified objects were alike. Objects in this test might include things like potato and carrot, or cat and mouse, and so on.

The first of the non-verbal tests was *Pattern Meanings*. In this test the child being tested was required to suggest as many interpretations of a series of abstract designs, drawn on cards and given to him to examine, as possible. *Line Meanings* was a very similar test in that the child was presented with a card on which was a line. He was asked to suggest as many interpretations of the line as he could think of. Each line was a single continuous unit and it is in this respect that the *Line Meanings* test differs from the *Pattern Meanings* test. In the latter test, the elements of the stimulus patterns were discrete and not connected.

SCORING OF WALLACH AND KOGAN TESTS

In all cases, two scores were derived from the children's responses to the various tests. These scores were for uniqueness, and for number of responses. The uniqueness score was obtained by noting the number of answers given by a particular child to a particular item which were quite unique, within the whole group. Thus, this score indicates how many responses were given by the child concerned which were given by no other member of the total group tested. The number of responses score closely resembled the fluency score described by Torrance, in that it was obtained by simply counting the total number of suggestions offered for any item.

Although these tests look very much like the tests described in earlier sections, Wallach and Kogan report important differences in some of the properties of scores they yielded. In the first place, the five tests correlated very highly with each other, but showed very low cross-correlations with convergent measures which were also administered to the children involved in the study. Furthermore, reliabilities of the tests, calculated by a short-cut method which avoids having to give the tests twice over, were very high indeed, sometimes as high as ·93, which indicates the likelihood of almost perfect agreement between a given child's scores if he took the tests on two occasions. In both these respects, the Wallach and Kogan tests differ markedly from other creativity tests, possibly because of the different administrational procedures. This increased factorial validity and reliability, which characterises the more recent battery, suggests that these tests will prove to be the most valuable in future investigation in the area of creativity. However, it is unlikely that the work of Guilford and Torrance will be completely disregarded, especially in view of the heavily derivative nature of Wallach and Kogan's tests.

References

ANDERSON, C. C., and CROPLEY, A. J. (1966). 'Some correlates of originality', *Aust. J. Psychol.* **18,** 218–227.

ANDERSON, J. E. (1960). 'The nature of abilities', in Torrance, E. P., ed. *Education and talent.* Minneapolis: University of Minnesota Press.

ANDREWS, E. G. (1930). 'The development of imagination in the pre-school child', *University of Iowa studies in character* **3.**

BARKAN, M. (1960). *Through art to creativity.* Boston: Allyn and Bacon.

BARRON, F. (1955). 'The disposition towards originality', *J. abnorm. soc. Psychol.* **51,** 478–85.

BARRON, F. (1963). *Creativity and psychological health.* New York: Van Nostrand.

BARTLETT, F. (1958). *Thinking.* New York: Basic Books.

BIGGS, J. B. (1965). 'Towards a psychology of educative learning', *Inter. Rev. Educ.* **11,** 77–93.

BRUNER, J. S. (1957). 'On going beyond the information given', in *Contemporary approaches to cognition.* Cambridge, Mass.: Harvard University Press.

BRUNER, J. S. (1962). 'The creative surprise', in Gruber, H. E., Terrell, G. and Wortheimer, M., eds. *Contemporary approaches to creative thinking.* New York: Atherton Press.

BRUNER, J. S. and OLVER, R. R. (1963). 'The development of equivalence transformations in children', in Wright, J. C. and Kagan, J., eds. 'Basic cognitive processes in children'. *Child Develpm. Monogr.* No. 86, 28.

CLIFFORD, P. I. (1958). 'Emotional contacts with the external world manifested by selected groups of highly creative chemists and mathematicians', *Percept. mot. Skills,* Monogr. Suppl. No. 1, **8,** 3–26.

CLINE, V. B., RICHARDS, J. M. and NEEDHAM, W. E. (1963). 'Creativity tests and achievement in high school science', *J. appl. Psychol.* **47,** 184–9.

CROPLEY, A. J. (1965). 'Originality, intelligence and personality.' Unpublished doctoral dissertation, University of Alberta.

CROPLEY, A. J. (1966). 'Creativity and intelligence,' *Brit. J. educ. Psychol.* **36,** 259–266).

CROPLEY, A. J. (1967). 'Creativity, intelligence, and achievement', *Alta. J. educ. Res.* (in press).

CRUTCHFIELD, R. S. (1955). 'Conformity and character', *Amer. Psychologist* **10,** 191–8.

DENTLER, R. A. and MACKLER, B. (1964). 'Originality: some social and personal determinants', *Behavioural Science* **9,** 1–7.

DREVDAHL, J. E. (1964). 'Some developmental and environmental factors in creativity', in Taylor, C. W., ed. *Widening horizons in creativity.* New York: Wiley.

DREVDAHL, J. E. and CATTELL, R. B. (1958). 'Personality and creativity in artists and writers', *J. clin. Psychol.* **14,** 107–11.

EIDUSON, B. T. (1958). 'Artist and non-artist: A comparative study', *J. Pers.* **26,** 13–28.

FREUD, S. (1910). *Leonardo da Vinci: A study in psychosexuality.* New York: Random House, 1947.

GARWOOD, D. S. (1964). 'Personality factors related to creativity in young scientists', *J. abnorm. soc. Psychol.* **68,** 413–19.

GETZELS, J. W. and JACKSON, P. W. (1962). *Creativity and intelligence.* New York: Wiley.

GHISELIN, B. (1955). *The creative process.* New York: Mentor Books.

GOERTZEL, V. and GOERTZEL, M. G. (1962). *Grades of eminence.* Boston: Little Brown.

GORDON, W. J. (1961). *Synectics.* New York: Harper Bros.

GUILFORD, J. P. (1950). 'Creativity', *Amer. Psychologist* **5,** 444–54.

GUILFORD, J. P. (1959). 'Three faces of intellect', *Amer. Psychologist* **14,** 469–79.

HEBB, D. O. (1949). *The organisation of behaviour.* New York: Wiley.

HELSON, R. (1966). 'Personality of women with imaginative and artistic interests: the role of masculinity, originality, and other characteristics in their creativity', *J. Pers.* **34,** 1–25.

HOBELMAN, L. (1957). 'Three creative teachers', *Clearing House,* **32,** 161–2.

HOLLAND, J. L. (1959). 'Some limitations of teacher ratings as predictors of creativity', *J. educ. Psychol.* **50,** 219–23.

HUDSON, L. (1963). 'Personality and scientific apitude', *Nature, Lond.* **196,** 913–14.

HUDSON, L. (1966). *Contrary imaginations.* London: Methuen.

KNELLER, G. F. (1965). *The art and science of creativity.* New York: Holt, Rinehart and Winston.

KOESTLER, A. (1964). *The act of creation.* London: Hutchinson.

KOGAN, N. and WALLACH, M. A. (1964). *Risk taking: A study in cognition and personality.* New York: Holt, Rinehart and Winston.

LURIA, A. R. (1961). *The role of speech in the regulation of normal and abnormal behaviour.* New York: Pergamon Press.

MCCLELLAND, D. C. (1958). 'Issues in the identification of talent', in McClelland, D. C., Baldwin, A. L., Bronfenbrenner, U. and Strodtbeck, F. L., eds. *Talent and society*. Princeton: Van Nostrand.

MCCLELLAND, D. C. (1963) 'The calculated risk: an aspect of scientific performance', in Taylor, C. W. and Barron F., eds. *Scientific creativity: its recognition and development*. New York: Wiley.

MCCLOY, W. and MEIER, N. C. (1931). 'Re-creative imagination', *Psychol. Monogr.* **51,** 108–16.

MACKINNON, D. W. (1962). 'The nature and nurture of creative talent', *Amer. Psychologist* **17,** 484–95.

MACKLER, B. (1962). 'Creativity and life styles.' Unpublished doctoral dissertation, University of Kansas.

MALTZMAN, I. (1960). 'On the training of originality', *Psychol. Rev.* **67,** 229–42.

MALTZMAN, I., BOGARTZ, W. and BREGER, L. (1958). 'A procedure for increasing word association originality and its transfer effects', *J. exp. Psychol.* **56,** 392–8.

MALTZMAN, I., SIMON, S., RASKIN, D. and LICHT, L. (1960). 'Experimental studies in the training of originality', *Psychol. Monogr.* **6,** (Whole No. 493).

MEDNICK, S. A. (1962). 'The associative basis of creativity', *Psychol. Rev.* **69,** 220–32.

MEER, B. and STEIN, M. I. (1955). 'Measures of intelligence and creativity', *J. Psychol.* **39,** 117–26.

MOORE, O. K. (1961). 'Orthographic symbols and the pre-school child—a new approach', in Torrance, E. P., ed. *New educational ideas: Second Minnesota conference on gifted children*. Minneapolis: Centre for continuation study.

NICHOLS, R. C. and HOLLAND, J. L. (1963). 'Prediction of the first year college performance of high aptitude students', *Psychol. Monogr.* **77,** 1–29.

ORNSTEIN, J. A. (1961). 'New recruits for science', *Parents' Mag.* **36,** 101–3.

OSGOOD, C. E. (1953). *Method and theory in experimental psychology*. New York: Oxford University Press.

PARNES, S. J. and MEADOW, A. (1959). 'Effects of brainstorming instructions on creative problem-solving by trained and untrained subjects', *J. educ. Psychol.* **50,** 171–6.

PARNES, S. J. and MEADOW, A. (1960). 'Evaluation of persistence of effects produced by a creative problem-solving course', *Psychol. Rep.* **7,** 357–61.

PARNES, S. J. and HARDING, H. F. (1962). *A sourcebook for creative thinking*. New York: Scribners.

PETTIGREW, T. F. (1958). 'The measurement and correlates of category width as a cognitive variable', *J. Pers.* **26,** 532–44.

POINCARE, H. (1913). 'Mathematical creation', in Poincare, H., ed. *The foundation of science.* New York: Science Press.

PRIBRAM, K. H. (1964). 'Neurological notes on the art of educating', in Hilgard, E. R., ed. *NSSE Yrbook.*, LXIII. Chicago: University of Chicago Press.

RICHARDS, J. M., CLINE, V. B. and NEEDHAM, W. E. (1964). 'Creativity tests and teacher and self judgements of originality', *J. exp. Educ.* **32,** 281–5.

RIPPLE, R. E. and MAY, F. (1962). 'Caution in comparing creativity and IQ', *Psychol. Rep.* **10,** 229–30.

ROE, A. (1963). 'Psychological approaches to creativity in science', in Coler, M. A., ed. *Essays on creativity in the sciences.* New York: New York University Press.

ROSSMAN, J. (1931). *The psychology of the inventor: a study of the patentee.* Washington: Inventors' Publishing Co.

SCHAEFFER, E. S. and BELL, R. Q. (1958). 'Development of a parent attitude research instrument', *Child Develpm.* **29,** 339–61.

SHARPE, E. F. (1950). *Collected papers on psychoanalysis.* London: Hogarth.

SKAGER, R. W., SCHULTZ, C. B. and KLEIN, S. P. (1965). 'Quality and quantity of accomplishment as measures of creativity', *J. educ. Psychol.* **56,** 31–9.

SIMPSON, R. M. (1922). 'Creative imagination', *Amer. J. Psychol.* **33,** 234–5.

STEIN, M. I. (1963). 'A transactional approach to creativity', in Taylor, C. W. and Barron, F., eds. *Scientific creativity: its discovery and development.* New York: Wiley.

SUCHMAN, J. R. *Elementary School training program in scientific inquiry.* Urbana: University of Illinois (mimeographed).

TAYLOR, C. W. (1964) ed. *Creativity: progress and potential.* New York: Wiley.

TERMAN, L. M. (1925). *Genetic studies of genius.* Stanford: Stanford University Press.

TORRANCE, E. P. (1959). *Explorations in creative thinking in the early school years: VIII. IQ and creativity in school achievement.* Minneapolis: Bur. educ. Res., University of Minnesota.

TORRANCE, E. P. (1960). *Educational achievement of the highly intelligent and the highly creative: Eight partial replications of the Getzels-Jackson study.* Minneapolis: Bur. educ. Res., University of Minnesota.

TORRANCE, E. P. (1961). 'Priming creative thinking in the primary grades', *Elementary School J.* **62,** 34–41.

TORRANCE, E. P. (1962a). *Guiding creative talent.* Englewood Cliffs: Prentice Hall.

TORRANCE, E. P. (1962b). 'Developing creative thinking through school experiences', in Parnes, S. J. and Harding, H. F., eds. *A sourcebook for creative thinking.* New York: Scribners.

TORRANCE, E. P. (1963). *Education and the creative potential.* Minneapolis: University of Minnesota Press.

TORRANCE, E. P. (1964). 'Education and creativity', in Taylor, C. W., ed. *Creativity: Progress and potential.* New York: McGraw–Hill.

TORRANCE, E. P. (1965a). *Rewarding creative behaviour.* Englewood Cliffs: Prentice Hall.

TORRANCE, E. P. (1965b). *Gifted children in the classroom.* New York: Macmillan.

TORRANCE, E. P. (1966). 'A strange road to the truth', *Contemporary Psychol.* **11,** 22–6.

TOYNBEE, A. (1962). 'Has America neglected its creative minority', *Calif. Monogr.* **72,** 7–10.

TYSON, M. 'Creativity', in Foss, B. M., ed. *New horizons in psychology.* London: Pelican.

VERNON, P. E. (1964). 'Creativity and intelligence', *Educ. Res.* **6,** 163–9.

WALLACH, M. A. and CARON, A. J. (1959). 'Attribute criteriality and sex-linked conservatism as determinants of psychological similarity', *J. Pers.* **59,** 43–50.

WALLACH, M. A. and KOGAN, N. (1965). *Modes of thinking in young children.* New York: Holt, Rinehart and Winston.

WEISBERG, P. S. and SPRINGER, K. J. (1961). 'Environmental factors in creative function', *Arch. gen. Psychiat.* **5,** 554–64.

WELCH, L. (1946). 'Recombination of ideas in creative thinking', *J. appl. Psychol.* **30,** 638–43.

WESSEL, H. M. (1961). 'Four teachers I have known', *Sat. Rev.* **44,** 58–9.

WITKIN, H. A. (1954). *Personality through perception.* New York: Harper.

WODTKE, K. H. (1964). 'Some data on the reliability and validity of creativity tests at the elementary school level', *Educ. psychol. Measmt.* **24,** 399–408.

YAMAMOTO, K. (1963). 'Relationships between creative thinking abilities of teachers and achievement and adjustment of pupils', *J. exp. Educ.* **32,** 3–25.

YAMAMOTO, K. (1964a). 'The role of creative thinking and intelligence in high school achievement', *Psychol. Rep.* **14,** 783–9.

YAMAMOTO, K. (1964b). 'A further analysis of the role of creative thinking in high school achievement', *J. Psychol.* **58,** 277–83.

YAMAMOTO, K. (1964c). 'Threshold of intelligence in academic achievement of highly creative students', *J. exp. Educ.* **32,** 401–5.

Index